Entertaining *Chic!*

Modern French Recipes & Table Settings for All Occasions

Entertaining *Chic!*

Modern French Recipes & Table Settings for All Occasions

Claudia Taittinger

Text by Lavinia Branca Snyder
Photography by Mark Roskams

RIZZOLI NEW YORK

New York · Paris · London · Milan

Contents

Preceding pages Château de la Marquetterie of the House of Taittinger is situated in the wine-growing village of Pierry. *Opposite* The interplay of colors and the flower motif are the foundation for the joyful theme that evokes a summer table in a garden. The pink digitalis foxgloves add a romantic touch to the scene. *Following pages* Dinner is set in the Montmartre studio of the artist Ruben Alterio, where candles provide a simple decorative focus. The white candles—assembled in a seemingly random pattern—shed a golden light and create a feeling of intimacy and warmth that contrast with the Parisian streetscape seen through the studio's expansive windows.

Introduction

The instance that lingers in our memory years later is a musical note, a mood. The flavors and aromas of that luncheon or dinner that we fondly recall are a performance, if you will. An artifice created through a combination of location, food selections, the nominal occasion, and, of course, the guests in attendance.

When entertaining at home it is the "where" and the "who" that become the pillars upon which a host, or hostess, can build a truly memorable repast. Each home's location, and the guests that are expected, provide the inspiration for the host to create a one-of-a-kind performance, where both stagecraft and culinary adventures play a part.

The goal is to affect two distinct realms: that of emotion and that of imagination—and to do so with a theatrical effect that will bring forth and mirror the warmth of human contact. The most successful seated dinner, luncheon, or more casual gathering is the one that achieves an intertwining of both.

Whether hosting a larger get-together or an intimate dinner over the flickering light of candles, it all comes down to a harmonious mood and the excitement of surprises, created by the chosen elements as devised by the host.

At the table, the elements that one can unveil include the decorative centerpieces and candles, as well as the choice of an elegant tablecloth and napkin set, or a more austere table where the cutlery, china, and glassware take center stage.

All should be selected with an overarching view as to the effect one seeks to enhance in the planned formal luncheon, intimate supper, or country gathering. Small gatherings of up to six people are more prone to intimacy, while gatherings of eight and up are ripe for surprises and dramatic denouements.

This performance, much like life, evolves in a span of space and time as the dishes are presented; its flow entices the participants to become part of the performance. The meal is thus the distillation of a single moment in time, as well as the expression of a place, its people, its traditions, its culinary culture, and the produce of its land.

Within these parameters one is guided by traditional, and some new, rules of etiquette that are the modern framework of the *art de la table*.

Opposite A beautiful moss-covered stone pedestal table is decorated with red roses and poached peaches. The bucolic repast is laid out against the elegant façade of Château de la Marquetterie of the House of Taittinger. *Following pages* The design of the Mottahedeh Merian service was inspired by the scientist and artist Maria Sibylla Merian, who is best known for her 1685 volume of botanical and entomological illustrations. Twenty-three separate colors as well as gold filigree are present in each flower design.

France at the Queen's Elm

Of Napoleon & Queen Elizabeth I

The pale English sunlight streams through the windowpanes of this London home, cascading onto the green and gray tablecloth to create a spring-like tableau; it heightens the nuances of the centerpieces of natural greenery, while bringing to life the acid-green balloton glasses displayed on the dining table.

"Let us be masters of the Channel for six hours and we are masters of the world," declared Napoleon of his planned invasion of the United Kingdom.

Although no invasion came to pass, in the two centuries after the tabling of these plans, London became one of the world's most international cities: a vibrant and cosmopolitan urban capital that resonates with the accent and the imported customs of its many French residents.

When Boris Johnson was mayor of London, he quipped to France's former prime minister, Alain Juppé, that he had the honor of representing 250,000 French citizens living in London, which made him the mayor of the sixth-largest French city on earth!

At the very heart of London's Borough Chelsea, in an area where many French residents have their homes, we find Queen's Elm Square. The square was built in a horseshoe shape around the spot where Queen Elizabeth I is said to have sheltered from the rain under an elm tree with Lord Burghley. The "Queen's Tree" was recorded as early as 1586 and soon thereafter an arbor was built around it.

Designed in a Tudor-revival style, this home features timber-framed walls filled in with lath and plaster, as well as the brick chimneys and tiled roofs that were mandated by the city in the thirteenth century to reduce the threat of fires. While its architecture is a celebration of London's Tudor past, its decorative interiors, the lifestyle and dining preferences, all mirror its Gallic allegiance.

From the striped French lampshades to the Orientalist wallpaper; from the busts of Napoleon prominently displayed on the dining room side table to the classic "L'Instant Taittinger" poster; from the delicate langoustines to the morel mushrooms and the chocolate cakes, everything speaks of a great love of country.

Although not quite the invasion that Napoleon sought, in this home France has, indeed, planted its flag!

A vintage Taittinger poster and the Beauvillé pale green and gray paisley tablecloth are brought together to create a sophisticated country flair in the patio dining room. The Nason Moretti acid-green water glasses, crafted in Murano, provide a visual spark that brings out the spring-like green tones of the room.

Zucchini Soup
Serves 8

Ingredients

2 large shallots, chopped
1 clove garlic, chopped
1 tablespoon unsalted butter or extra virgin olive oil
4 large zucchini/courgettes, washed and cut into slices
1 potato, cut into thin slices (optional)
2 cups (500 ml) chicken broth
Leaves of 1 small bunch basil or cilantro/coriander, plus more for garnish
Knob of butter, for serving
Crème fraîche or olive oil, for serving

Preparation

In a large pot, sauté the shallots and garlic with the butter over medium heat, stirring constantly until the shallots are transparent, 3 minutes.
Add the sliced zucchini and the potato slices, if using. Continue to stir.
Add the chicken broth and bring to a simmer.
Let simmer on low for 7 minutes.
Immediately blend with an immersion/stick blender or pour the mixture into a standing blender, in batches, if necessary, as the contents are hot, so the vegetables stay green.
When smooth, blend in the basil. Return the contents to the pot.
Stir in a knob of butter and serve topped with crème fraîche or olive oil and fresh basil leaves.

Preceding pages The wood tones and walnut cross-back chairs combine with green and floral decorative accents to convey a sense of timelessness and warmth to the patio dining room. *Above* The Meissen porcelain soup cup and saucer are hand-painted and feature green leaves and flower decorations with a gold trim. They are placed on the larger, green Bernardaud Constance dinner plate.

Dressed Crab
Serves 6

Ingredients

Flesh of 2 avocados
Kernels from 1 ear cooked sweet corn
2 tablespoons freshly squeezed lemon juice
Salt
3/4 pound (350 g) crab or king crab meat
or cooked shrimp/prawns
1 tablespoon mayonnaise
Pepper
1 tablespoon chopped cilantro/coriander leaves,
chopped chives, and chopped parsley, plus more
whole leaves for serving
Crab claws, for serving (optional)
Baby greens, for serving
Mayonnaise, for serving (optional)
Lime quarters, for serving (optional)

Preparation

In a medium bowl, thoroughly mash the avocado,
then stir in the corn, 1 tablespoon of the lemon juice,
and salt.
In a small bowl, mix the crab, mayonnaise, the remaining tablespoon of lemon juice, salt, pepper, and herbs.
Place a single-serving (2 1/2- to 3-inch/6- to 7 1/2-cm)
round ring mold on a serving plate. Fill the bottom of
the circle with the avocado mixture and top with the
seasoned crabmeat. Remove the ring and repeat for
the remaining servings.
Decorate with crab claws or whole coriander leaves
and serve with baby greens. Mayonnaise and lime
quarters can be served on the side.

19

The Alberto Pinto foliage plate is hand-painted in France on fine white porcelain and makes
for a striking contrast to Zulu plate chargers fabricated of recycled telephone wire!

Above The unusual table centerpiece in the upstairs dining room is an exemplar of a rare antique avian taxidermy grouping that lends a naturalistic color palette to the rich golden tones of the table. *Opposite* The ochre tones of the satin tablecloth parallel the golden hues of the Bohemian cut glass and the yellow handblown stemware. This assemblage of warm colors creates a perfect visual harmony with the chestnut tones of this beamed room.

Blanquette de Veau

Serves 8

Ingredients

For the Veal
2 carrots
2 cloves garlic
2 large stalks celery
3 shallots
2 large onions
4 whole cloves
2 white leeks
3 1/3 pounds (1.5 kg) veal shoulder or flank,
cut into 2-inch (5-cm) pieces
2 small veal osso buco bones, optional
1 bouquet garni (a few sprigs thyme and rosemary;
2 bay leaves)
Stalks of 1 small bunch flat-leaf parsley
1 tablespoon sea salt
1 teaspoon peppercorns

For the Sauce
5 1/2 tablespoons (80 g) unsalted butter
4 tablespoons all-purpose/plain flour
1 cup (250 ml) heavy cream or crème fraîche

For Finishing
12 soaked dried morels (or 14 ounces/400 g small white
button mushrooms)
2 tablespoons unsalted butter
Salt
4 carrots
1 teaspoon sugar
1 tablespoon freshly squeezed lemon juice
Grated nutmeg
Boiled potatoes, rice, or pasta, for serving
Parsley leaves, for serving

Preparation

Peel the carrots, garlic, celery stalks, shallots, and onions.
Cut the onions in two and stud cloves into the onion halves.
Cut the carrots, shallots, and leeks into 1-inch (2 1/2-cm) pieces.
Rinse the meat and bones thoroughly in cold water.
Put the meat in a deep pot and cover with cold water (about
12 1/2 cups or 3 liters). Bring to a boil, uncovered, for 1 minute
and then drain the meat, rinse it under cold water, and
discard the cooking water; rinse the pot. Replace the meat
in the rinsed pot.
Add the vegetables, the bouquet garni, the parsley stalks,
the sea salt, and peppercorns. Add water to cover the meat.
Cook, uncovered, for at least 1 1/2 hours. When the meat is
tender, strain the contents of the pot through a sieve set over
a bowl; reserve the cooking broth.
Clean all the meat pieces and set aside.

Wash the pot and melt the butter with the flour to make
a roux. Cook over low heat, whisking constantly, for
5 minutes until the roux is pale golden.
Let the roux cool slightly and gradually add the reserved
cooking broth. Whisk over medium heat until it thickens
to a creamy consistency, then stir in the cream, add the
meat, and keep warm without boiling.

Drain the morels (or peel the button mushrooms) and sauté
them with a knob of butter and salt in a small nonstick
saucepan for about 5 minutes, until browned.
Peel the carrots and cut the carrots into 1/2-inch (1 1/4-cm)
rounds and place in a medium saucepan with water to cover,
salt, 1 teaspoon sugar, and knob of butter. Cook until tender,
about 15 minutes.
Transfer the mushrooms and carrots to the pot with the meat
and sauce, and stir in the lemon juice and a dash of grated
nutmeg. Serve with boiled potatoes, rice, or pasta topped
with a few parsley leaves.

Opposite The delicate aroma and texture of the boiled potatoes lend a perfect counterpoint
to the surprising texture of the morel mushrooms and the subtle richness of the veal gravy.
Following pages Changing the color palette of the patio dining table from the cooler
green palette to the warm reds creates an entirely different mood in the room.

Fondant au Chocolat
Serves 6

Ingredients

1 1/3 (150 g) sticks unsalted butter, plus more
for greasing
7 ounces (200 g) dark chocolate (60% cacao)
2/3 cup (150 g) superfine (caster) sugar
3 eggs
1/3 cup (50 g) all-purpose/plain flour
Berries, for serving
Ice cream or crème fraîche, for serving

Preparation

Butter 6 ramekins; set aside.
Microwave the butter for about 10 seconds,
until softened. Chop the chocolate and melt
in a bain-marie or double boiler.
In a bowl, combine the softened butter and sugar.
Add the eggs, one at a time, alternating with the flour.
Stir in the melted chocolate, pour the mixture into
buttered ramekins.
Put the ramekins in the freezer for 1 hour.
Preheat the oven to 300°F (150°C) and put the ramekins
in the oven for exactly 20 minutes. Unmold and serve hot,
decorated with berries and crème fraîche or ice cream.

The dark chocolate fondant is topped with vanilla ice cream and served with an assortment of seasonal berries on a white china plate. The deliberate contrast enhances the color impact of the rich chocolate and the berries. Cacao, originating from South America, was believed by the Aztecs to be a gift from the god of wisdom. In fact, the word chocolate comes from the Aztec word *xocoatl*. It was not until the sixteenth century, when the Spanish introduced cocoa to Europe, that sugar was added to it and it became popular throughout high society.

28

Lentil Soup

Serves 8

Ingredients

2 carrots
1 small onion
1 clove garlic
3 tablespoons olive oil
2 cups (400 g) green Puy lentils
8 cups vegetable broth
1/2 teaspoon ground cumin
Heavy cream, for serving (optional)
Leaves of 1 large handful parsley, coarsely chopped, and
olive oil, for serving (optional)

Preparation

Wash and peel the carrots and cut into large pieces.
Chop the onion and garlic.
In a casserole (or large saucepan), add the oil and sauté
the carrots, the onion, and the garlic until the onions
are translucent, about 3 minutes. Add the lentils and
the vegetable broth. Cook, covered, over medium heat
for about 30 minutes.
Once the vegetables are cooked, add the ground cumin
and stir. Remove and set aside 1 cup of the cooking liquid.
Puree with an immersion/stick blender until you have
a nice homogeneous soup, and adjust the consistency
with the cooking liquid to achieve your preferred level
of thickness (it's best between liquid and velvety thick).
To serve, top with a dash of cream or chopped parsley
and olive oil.

Chesnut Soup

Serves 6

Ingredients

3 shallots
2 cups olive oil
25 ounces (700 g) cooked chestnuts, chopped
3 cups beef broth
1/4 teaspoon grated nutmeg
Salt and pepper
About 1 cup milk
Sour cream, for serving
Chopped chives or bacon bits, for serving

Preparation

Chop the shallot and place in a large saucepan with the
olive oil. Sauté for 2 to 3 minutes, stirring constantly.
Add the chopped chestnuts, the beef broth, the nutmeg,
and salt and pepper as needed. Cook for 5 minutes.
Puree with an immersion/stick blender until very smooth
and velvety. Add the milk according to the consistency
you like. Adjust the seasoning with salt and pepper.
Serve the soup topped with a little sour cream
and chopped chives.

A close-up of the candles, artichokes, eggplants, and violet Bohemian cut-crystal glassware reveals the depth of
this sophisticated table décor. The contrasting green dinnerware offers a lovely frame for the cream of lentil soup.

Fleur de Sel

Dust of the Sea

Salt is no longer a costly and rare commodity, yet connoisseurs and chefs around the world still view one salt as a culinary treasure. It is France's fleur de sel, which translates to "flower of the salt." Thanks to trace calcium and magnesium chlorides that absorb moisture and give it a highly salty and complex flavor, it is said to taste like the ocean.

This gem is harvested in the salt drying pans found along France's northern Atlantic Coast. The most famous are in Guérande in the Loire-Atlantique, close to Brittany, as well as on the Island of Noirmoutier and the Île de Ré. These hand-harvested crystals rise to the top of the saltpans that hold the drying sea salt. The fleur de sel alone creates the perfect balance in *os à moelle* (grilled marrow).

In this beautiful port of Zapallar in Chile, on the Pacific Ocean, the ocean's spray scatters sparkling crystals on all it finds, seemingly oblivious to the heroic past of this humble mineral. Unseen and yet ever-present, this is the gift that Pablo Neruda evokes so beautifully in his poem, "Ode to Salt," "Dust of the sea, in you the tongue receives a kiss from ocean night . . ."

In fact, this life-sustaining nutrient was also a currency prized above all else in ancient times. Salt was used for the preservation of food for both the richest and the most humble of households, most significantly in winter and wartime. To wit, Roman soldiers were paid for their services with a *salarium argentum*, or rations of salt (along with other items and some money); hence the modern word salary.

On this impossibly clear day, as we prepare to feast on the riches of land and sea, the gentle sound of the waves gliding over the rocks fills the air; the rhythmic tide leaves behind a glistening coating of salt on the pebbles of the beach beneath us.

Far away the Pacific's blue horizon seems to almost disappear into the sky. In "It Is Born," Neruda writes, "Here I came to the very edge where nothing at all needs saying, everything is absorbed through weather and the sea."

In this sheltered cove where all is tranquility and harmony, lunch is served with a selection
of the famed Chilean rosé wines, as well as a bottle of chilled Taittinger.

Fried Fish with Caper Sauce
Serves 6

Ingredients

For the Fish
6 (6-ounce/170-g) fish fillets
(preferably white and skinless)
1/2 cup (60 g) all-purpose/plain flour
Vegetable oil for deep-frying
French fries or mashed potatoes and salad, for serving

For the Sauce
1 tablespoon butter
1 clove garlic, peeled and minced
1 tablespoon all-purpose/plain flour
1/2 cup (120 ml) lemon juice
1/2 cup (69 g) capers
1 cup (250 ml) water
Chopped parsley leaves

Preparation

For the Fish
Roll the fish fillets in flour. Pat the fillets to remove
the excess flour.
Deep-fry the fish in very hot vegetable oil until
golden brown.
Serve the fish hot with the Caper Sauce (recipe below).
Alternatively, serve with tartar sauce. You can serve
with French fries or mashed potatoes, and salad.

For the Suace
In a small saucepan, melt the butter; add the
garlic and sauté.
Stir in the flour; continue stirring. Pour in the
lemon juice.
Whisk vigorously to avoid lumps. Add the capers
and water.

Opposite The shrimp harvested off the coast of Chile benefits from the cold waters and abundant nutrients found there. This gives the crustaceans an unparalleled flavor. Grilling the entire batch in their shells results in a flavorful and moist meat. *Above* A classic French salad of tomatoes and onions served with mashed potatoes perfectly complements, in both flavors and texture, the sautéed fish caught earlier in the day.

Porotos Granados / Chilean Bean Casserole

Serves 8

Ingredients

3 1/3 pounds (1 1/2 kg) fresh cranberry beans
in their pods
Kernels of 3 ears corn or 2 1/4 cups frozen corn
1 small pumpkin or other winter squash
4 sprigs fresh basil
Paprika, pepper, and ground cumin to taste
3 tablespoons vegetable oil
2 medium onions, chopped
1 clove garlic, minced
Salt
Hot red pepper sauce, for serving
8 grilled pork sausages, for serving

Preparation

Shell the beans. Chop the corn. (If you prefer a thicker
texture to the final dish, puree about half of the corn with a
blender and chop the other half.) Seed and peel the pumpkin
and cut into 1/2-inch (1 1/4-cm) dice. Chop about 1 tablespoon of the leaves from 1 sprig basil. Set aside the remaining
leaves of that sprig for garnish.
Heat the oil in a large pot. Add the onion, garlic, and
chopped basil. Season with paprika, pepper, and cumin
and sauté for 5 minutes.
Add the beans and enough hot water to cover the beans
by several inches.
Add the pumpkin and 3 sprigs basil. Season to taste with salt.
Cook over medium heat for 15 minutes.
Add the corn and cook for 5 additional minutes.
Garnish with reserved basil and serve with hot red pepper
sauce and grilled pork sausages.

A Chilean countryside stew made with cranberry beans, corn kernels, and squash. This dish is an
ode to Chile's abundant vegetable harvest and is cooked in a clay casserole pot from Pomaire.

Above The bone is cut the long way so the marrow is fully exposed to the flame and is grilled over its entire length. It slowly acquires its outer crunchy crustiness as the fat is grilled. The newly created surface layer, and the grilled bread served with this dish, are the perfect accents to appreciate its interior fattiness. *Opposite* When fully cooked, the grilled or broiled bone marrow becomes soft, tastes very mild, and has absorbed the flavors and fragrance of the herbs and spices with which it was cooked.

Montmartre
The Past & the Now

In the edifice once occupied by Renoir, the evocative studio of Ruben Alterio speaks to the deepest yearnings of the artist's soul. Against this eclectic and vibrant cultural background, the menu parallels the Montmartre dynamic in the meeting of the traditional Vitel Tonne with the innovative chicory that is known as friseline.

To this day, Montmartre remains an old favorite of Parisians and foreigners alike. Nothing compares to walking up and down the crowded, quixotic, and charming streets of la Butte. One might be forgiven for not knowing that until it was annexed by the city of Paris in 1860, Montmartre was a quiet countryside area where vineyards and mills dotted the landscape.

Once this "annexation" took place, change occurred rapidly and soon this village within a city became the epicenter of the late-nineteenth-century bohemian life, where the hustle and bustle of its citizens, its lively smoky cafes, its cabaret performers, as well as the many artists and their muses, fostered an entirely new cultural life.

Poets and artists flocked to this place where anything was possible. Almost overnight, Le Chat Noir, the first modern cabaret, as well as the Lapin Agile and the Moulin Rouge, took over its nightlife with ever more elaborate and innovative performances, where artists such as Toulouse-Lautrec immortalized its most famous performers. The creative soul had found its home in Montmartre, and soon the studios of the Bateau-Lavoir became the place to discover its newest residents such as Le Douanier Rousseau, Picasso, and Modigliani.

Vitel Tonné's origin dates to the 1700s when it was first prepared in Italy's Piedmont region. "Vitel" is an abbreviation of the Italian word for veal; while "Tonné" is a Frenchified word that, according to the historian Giovanni Ballarini, refers to its cooking method, which is similar to how one cooked tuna, not to the sauce component.

Indeed, it was Pellegrino Artusi who introduced the tuna in the sauce in 1891 in his tome *La Scienza in cucina e l'arte di mangiar bene*. From that day on, Vitello Tonnato has been a refined staple loved across continents. In contrast, the friseline chicory salad green dates to 2016 when it was first introduced in France after a seed improvement method that took twenty years to perfect. On this day the two meet!

There are two schools of thought about the proper way to cut a French baguette. One encourages slicing it diagonally with a serrated knife on a wooden cutting board; the other advocates breaking off a piece with one's hands and placing it on the table next to the dinner plate.

Above The artist Ruben Alterio (right) is seen seated at the table, with his dear friend Michel Taittinger. The artist's paintbrushes and the candlesticks of different styles and various materials interspersed with the artist's artwork are a creative interpretation of the classic centerpiece. However, in a nod to a more traditional lifestyle, the proper number of candles (one per diner) is "de rigueur." *Opposite* Friseline is now a very popular salad green in France. The breeding station Vilmorin developed it by crossbreeding several distinct chicory varieties using a new seed improvement process. The simple black slate table and the minimalist cutlery setting is reminiscent of the bohemian lifestyle, making this wonderful Montmartre studio still feel like a separate, timeless island within the city.

Vitello Tonnato
Serves 6

Ingredients

1 pound (500g) loin of veal
8 cups (2 liters) court-bouillon
Salt and pepper
2 egg yolks
1 teaspoon mustard
1 cup (250 ml) sunflower oil
1 tablespoon freshly squeezed lemon juice
10 anchovy fillets
5 1/4 ounces (150 g) tuna in olive oil
1 tablespoon capers
Caperberries, for serving
Salad greens, lamb's lettuce, or chicory, for serving

Preparation

Season the meat with salt and pepper before wrapping it tightly in plastic wrap (cling film).
In a large pot or Dutch oven, carefully place the meat in the simmering court-bouillon and cook for approximately 20 minutes. Turn off the heat and let it rest in the liquid for another 20 minutes. Refrigerate for 4 hours.
Make a classic mayonnaise with the egg yolks, mustard, and sunflower oil, whisking thoroughly until the sauce emulsifies. Add the lemon juice, anchovies, tuna, and capers then mix with an immersion/stick blender until smooth.
Slice the veal very thinly and place on a flat serving dish, covering the entire surface. Spread the sauce over the veal slices and garnish with caperberries. Serve with salad greens, lamb's lettuce, or chicory.

The plated meat of the vitello tonnato dish is presented thinly sliced
with, at its a center, a portion of the sauce topped by caperberries.

At the Boathouse

Fruits de Mer

The ocean offers us a seeming endless variety of seafood in curiously magical shapes and sizes. Those ocean inhabitants that are known as the fruits of the sea ("fruits de mer") are the eclectic princes among the kings of the deep. They are the crustaceans and the mollusks, and truly are a breed apart.

The display of the bounty of the sea that is taking form before us seems to expertly blur geographical boundaries. There's nothing like a banquet of fruits de mer to make us forget that we find ourselves far from France, on the Chilean coast, in a different hemisphere and continent, in a magical spot where the seasons are inverted.

First detailed in 1802, by the noted French zoologist Pierre-André Latreille in his *Histoire naturelle générale et particulière des crustacés et insectes* (*Comprehensive Natural History of Crustaceans and Insects*) the crustaceans and their mollusk counterparts have captivated and challenged both fishermen and chefs alike.

They have antennas and legs, hard shells, and hidden treasures of pearls; they have voluptuous sounding names like *moules* (mussels, or *mejillones* in Spanish); or rather fancy proper names like *coquille St Jacques* (scallop, or *vieira*) or are referred to by the elegant sounding *crevette* (shrimp, or *camarón*).

For as long as anyone can remember, the inhabitants of French cities, towns, and villages herald the start of the fall season with the ritual arrival of the ice-covered street displays of delicious shellfish known as fruits de mer.

Then, an unspoken but heartfelt competition pits humble fishmongers against storied brasseries, and fancy restaurants against each other, in a duel of aesthetic and culinary bravado with the ultimate goal to display the broadest palette, the freshest catch, and the best of the seasonal offerings of the sea.

Whether served simply steamed and then chilled on resplendent multitiered plateaus in Paris, or grilled over an open charcoal flame on a beach where the Humboldt Current feeds the Pacific, these small clams and giant blue crabs bring out the flavor and the memories of the best of times...

A casual late afternoon lunch is laid out on the pebble beach furnished
with a white dining table and traditional Roman design stools.

Clam & Chorizo Linguine

Serves 5

Ingredients

2 1/4 pounds (1 kg) clams (cockles, baby clams)
1 tablespoon olive oil
1 small spicy chorizo sausage, sliced thinly
2 cloves garlic, crushed
1/2 cup (120 ml) white wine
1 cup (240 ml) cream
1/2 cup chopped parsley leaves
1 pound (500 g) linguine

Preparation

Rinse the clams. Place them in a bowl of cold water for 1 hour. Let the sand settle at the bottom, then carefully remove the clams from the bowl with your hands. Place in a clean bowl. Meanwhile, heat the oil in a large sauté pan, add the chorizo, and cook until crisp.

Remove the chorizo from the pan using a slotted spoon. Add the crushed garlic, the clams, and white wine to the pan. Cook, covered, for about 3 minutes.

Stir and cook, uncovered, for another minute or so until the clams open (discard any that do not open). Add the crisp chorizo, the cream, and the chopped parsley. Keep covered and warm.

Cook the pasta in a large saucepan of boiling salted water and drain; reserve 1/2 cup of the cooking water. Add the pasta to the chorizo and clam mixture and toss gently to combine. Add some of the reserved cooking water if it seems too dry.

An Italian dish with a Latino twist, clams and chorizo sausage linguine is a favorite at family gatherings.

When paired with the rustic rattan placemats, the fiery coral motif of these
simple yet elegant plates provides a vibrant frame for the clam dish.

Due to the Humboldt Current, the Chilean Sea is considered among the most productive
marine ecosystems in the world. This afternoon, the wispy gray smoke cloud that rises
into the air carries with it the tantalizing aromas of this bounty.

Shrimp Pil Pil
Serves 4

Ingredients

4 cloves garlic
1/2 cup (100 ml) olive oil
1 pound (500 g) peeled jumbo shrimp
1 hot red pepper or 1/2 teaspoon ground
hot red pepper (merkén)
3/4 cup (180 ml) white wine
Salt and pepper
1/4 cup chopped fresh cilantro/coriander leaves

Preparation

Peel and crush the garlic. Heat the olive oil in a large sauté pan. Sauté the garlic and shrimp for 2 minutes. Add the ground red pepper cut in strips (or the hot red pepper) and the white wine. Cook both sides of the shrimp until pink and the wine has almost evaporated. Season with salt, pepper, and the chopped cilantro (coriander).

The Chilean barbecue consists of a metal grill, or parilla, suspended above a coal or wood fire. Cooking the shellfish directly over the charcoal in the heat-resistant clay cooking pots is an important part of the seaside barbecue.

Terrace with a View
Of Taste and Enjoyment

In the preface to his voluminous 1893 cookbook *The Epicurean*, Chef Charles Ranhofer professes to publish the book in order to provide the reader with "the best and most effectual manner of preparing healthy and nutritious food." This art and practice are the very heart of life along this wild and untamed stretch of coastline of the Chilean Pacific.

The *oeuf poché* (poached egg) made its first print appearance in Ranhofer's book, the masterpiece of the legendary Paris-trained chef, who made his name at Delmonico's in New York. It is considered a seminal publication that served to legitimize and systematize the culinary arts.

Poaching is a simple yet subtle cooking technique that uses moist heat to cook delicate-textured foods such as eggs, poultry, fish, or fruit in a liquid. It does so at a lower temperature than is used when simmering or boiling. This is done in order to preserve the moisture content and the integrity of the food being prepared.

Years later, Georges-Auguste Escoffier, known as the "king of chefs and chef of kings," famous for his innovation in all manners of French cuisine, listed over one hundred variations of oeufs pochés in his 1934 book *Ma Cuisine*. "Poché" is derived from the French word *poche* (pocket) that literally suggests that food is cooked as though placed in a pocket.

When another giant in the history of gastronomy, Prosper Montagné, published his *Larousse Gastronomique* in 1938, he provided the formulas for several poached-egg dishes, beginning with oeufs Aladin.

Finally, in 1976, Michel Guérard, a chef with three Michelin stars and credited as one of the founders of French Nouvelle Cuisine, plays with the possibilities of this cooking method when he flaunts the now widely adopted baked eggs steamed in water (*oeufs au plat à l'eau*).

He seems to address the very qualities of poaching as a cooking method in *The Essential Cuisine Minceur* when he suggests that his clean approach is squarely faithful to the idea that: "Taste and enjoyment are at the heart of all French cooking."

Certainly no one could imagine that such a humble food as an egg, delicately cooked in water, could be the inspiration to countless culinary masters and feed their creativity for centuries... even wrapping it in smoked salmon and standing it up in the fresh air....

A combination of mediums of artistic expression such as furniture, tableware, and food transforms the perception of what lies beyond and highlights the contrast in the evolution of life along the coastline of Valparaiso.

Eggs in Aspic
Serves 4

Ingredients

2 cups (500 ml) clear chicken or beef stock
1 packet unflavored gelatin powder or 2 gelatin leaves
(soaked in cold water and drained)
1 tablespoon Madeira wine
A few fresh tarragon leaves or capers
4 pasture-raised eggs
4 (2 x 7-inch/5 x 18-cm) strips cooked ham
or smoked salmon
Salad greens and herbs, for serving

Preparation

Bring the clear chicken stock to a boil. Add the unflavored
gelatin powder, mixing with a whisk for 1 minute.
Add the Madeira.
Pour a little of the gelatin into the bottom of 4 ramekins
or aspic molds. Carefully top with tarragon leaves or capers.
Place the ramekins in the refrigerator for about 15 minutes,
until set.
Poach the eggs for 6 minutes. You can also soft-boil the eggs,
then set them in cold water and carefully peel them.
Wrap each egg with a strip of ham or smoked salmon. Place
them on the set gelatin in the ramekins. Fill in with the rest
of the cool but still liquid gelatin. Refrigerate for 3 hours.
To unmold, dip the bottom of the ramekins in hot water for
a few seconds. Slip the blade of a knife inside the ramekins.
Serve with salad greens and herbs.

*Note: You can also serve this with a mayonnaise and herb sauce
(mix mayonnaise with fresh parsley, tarragon, dill, and basil).*

The small ceramic bowl known as a ramekin is used in the
preparation of this dish to create the desired shape for the gelée.

Opposite and Above The bold color contrast of the red table linen and the white chairs highlights the ocean seascape and lends a fresh and bold aesthetic to the set. The ocean crashes wildly beneath the terrace, sending the salt mist high above us and then gently cascading a few salt crystals onto the plates, adding its own special touch to our catch.

Salmon Teriyaki
Serves 8

Ingredients

1/4 cup (50 ml) soy sauce
1/4 cup (55 g) brown sugar
1/4 cup (50 ml) mirin
2 tablespoons rice vinegar
1 shallot, minced
2 cloves garlic, minced
1/2 teaspoon sambal oelek (red pepper paste)
1 side salmon, skin removed (about 6 pounds/3 kg)
1 tablespoon sesame seeds
1 tablespoon olive oil
Salt and pepper
Caramelized pumpkin cubes and cooked lentils,
for serving

Preparation

In a small saucepan, combine the soy sauce, brown sugar, mirin, vinegar, shallot, garlic, and sambal oelek. Bring to a boil. Simmer over medium heat for about 10 minutes, or until sauce is syrupy. Keep the sauce warm.
Sprinkle the top of the salmon with sesame seeds. In a large nonstick skillet over medium heat, warm the olive oil until hot. Cook the salmon, sesame-seed side down, for 3 minutes. Season with salt and pepper. Turn the salmon over and continue cooking for 3 minutes, or until the desired doneness. Place the salmon on a serving dish, top with the sauce, then garnish with the caramelized pumpkin cubes and cooked lentils.

One of the best ways to add heat and the flavor of chili pepper to a dish is with sambal oelek.
The paste has roots in Malaysian and Indonesian cooking and is prepared without sugar, vinegar,
and garlic. "Oelek" refers to a mortar and pestle–type device that's used to crush the ingredients.

Château de la Marquetterie
Pink Lights & Champagne

The Taittinger production offers a broad range of delicately aromatic wines. Their selection ranges from the Comtes de Champagne Blanc de Blancs, Taittinger's most prestigious wine, produced only with the best Grands Crus terroirs and vintages of Chardonnay, to its many innovative and creative blends of Chardonnay, Pinot Noir, and Pinot Meunier. Each wine has an elegant complexity that enhances any dish, whether it is the savory and subtle nuances found in a risotto or the delicate sweetness of poached fruits and Florentines.

Situated in the village of Pierry south of Epernay, the Château de la Marquetterie is the embodiment of the very spirit of Taittinger; its history is filled with the unpredictable vagaries of fate and yet steeped in the timeless traditions of the region.

The estate traces its history back to 1734, when the château was the home of the author Jacques Cazotte, whose *Le Diable Amoureux* is often said to be the first example of French "fantastique," a new literary genre that combined science fiction and supernatural fantasy.

In 1914, during World War I, Pierre-Charles Taittinger, a young cavalry officer, was stationed there when Marshal Joseph Joffre made the château his headquarters. Pierre-Charles Taittinger fell in love with the property and after the war he was able to purchase the house, as well as cellars that date back to the fourth century and finally the vineyards, considered to be some of the best in the Champagne region.

Owned by Pierre-Charles since 1934, and today still managed by his descendants, the Taittinger house has many fine wines, including Taittinger Brut Réserve, Brut Prestige Rosé, Brut Millésimé, Prélude "Grands Crus," Les Folies de la Marquetterie, Nocturne Sec, Comtes de Champagne Blanc de Blancs, Comtes de Champagne Rosé, and Taittinger Collection.

By the 1950s, the global appeal and the quality of Taittinger, coupled with its impeccable reputation, had earned it two very different accolades, each deserving of a mention.

Taittinger joined the *Union des Maisons de Champagne*, a syndicate of the best Champagne houses, which includes Bollinger, Laurent Perrier, Moët & Chandon, and Louis Roederer.

In 1953, Ian Fleming in chapter 8 of *Casino Royale*, his first novel featuring James Bond, introduces in his narrative Taittinger Champagne when, during a late dinner with Vesper Lynd, Bond describes it as "probably the finest Champagne in the world."

Côte des Blancs is the area in the Champagne region whose terroir is known as the most noble and conducive to providing the greatest of wines. Its composition is predominantly limestone and chalk, which is credited with giving the Comtes de Champagne Blanc de Blancs a great aromatic finesse and a structure that is quite out of the ordinary.

The centerpiece of grapes in a silver vessel sets the tone and color of the table décor and the linens.
Their understated palette is echoed in the Beauvillé tablecloth and the Roses de Tuscia Limoges
dinnerware designed by Nall for Robert Haviland and C. Parlon.

Champagne Risotto

Serves 8

Ingredients

2 shallots
2 cloves garlic
1/4 cup (60 ml) olive oil
2 1/2 cups Arborio rice
3 glasses Champagne
2 to 3 cups hot chicken broth
2 tablespoons (30 g) butter
2 tablespoons heavy cream
1 1/4 cups (100 g) grated Parmesan cheese
Freshly ground pink peppercorns
Truffle slices, for garnish (optional)
Chopped flat-leaf parsley leaves, for garnish (optional)

Preparation

Peel and chop the shallots, and peel and halve the garlic cloves. Heat the oil in a nonstick pan and sauté the chopped shallot and the garlic. Add the rice and sauté until the grains become opaque white. Add the champagne and let evaporate.

Add a ladle of broth and cook, stirring continuously, until the broth is absorbed, then add another ladle. Continue until the dish has the consistency of a creamy, heavy soup (if too thick, continue to add more broth). This should take 15 minutes. Remove the pan from the heat and discard the garlic.

Add the butter and stir, then add the cream, the grated Parmesan, and ground pepper. Stir to combine thoroughly. Garnish with truffle slices and chopped parsley.

Risotto is a northern Italian rice dish cooked with the gradual addition of broth until it reaches a creamy consistency. In this French adaptation, Champagne replaces the traditional white wine.

The Bernardaud Reine Elizabeth Limoges dinnerware was designed for the reception of Her Majesty Queen Elizabeth on the occasion of her visit to France in April 1957. It complements beautifully the crimson table décor of the wood-paneled dining room.

Turkey Paupiettes in Champagne Sauce

Serves 6

Ingredients

8 3/4 ounces (250 g) ground turkey (or chicken)
Salt and pepper
1 1/2 teaspoons ground dried sage or tarragon
6 pounded turkey fillets
6 slices smoked bacon
2 tablespoons vegetable oil
2 onions, peeled and finely chopped
2 cloves garlic, peeled and crushed
7 ounces (200 g) white mushrooms, sliced
1 cup (250 ml) Taittinger Champagne
1 tablespoon all-purpose/plain flour
2 cups (500 ml) chicken broth
2/3 cup (150 ml) heavy cream
Pearl onions, Brussels sprouts with bacon
and chestnuts, potatoes, or rice, for serving

Preparation

Season the ground turkey with salt, pepper, and ground sage. Spread each turkey fillet on a board. Put a spoonful of ground turkey in the middle, then fold up the sides to enclose the filling.

Wrap a slice of bacon around each paupiette and secure with a toothpick. Truss with kitchen twine to keep closed and to ensure the stuffing is completely covered.

Heat the oil in a sauté pan over high heat. Fry the paupiettes to brown them on all sides. Transfer the browned paupiettes to a platter and set aside.

In the same pan, fry the finely chopped onion and garlic. Add the mushrooms and salt and pepper and cook for 2 minutes. Add the Champagne and let reduce for 2 minutes. Remove the toothpicks.

Return the paupiettes to the pan with the sauce and sprinkle the flour on top. Add the chicken broth, stir well, cover, and let cook for 15 minutes. Add the cream and continue cooking, uncovered, for 5 minutes. The sauce will thicken and reduce. Remove twine and serve with pearl onions, Brussels sprouts, potatoes, or rice.

Opposite The term *paupiette* appears in *Suite des dons de Comus; ou L'art de la cuisine* by Francois Marin in 1762. The word and the recipe are a derivation of the Italian *polpette*, whose recipe and name Maestro Martino recorded some three centuries earlier in the famous *Libro de arte coquinaria* in 1460.
Following pages The perfect accompaniment to the poached fruit, the Florentine cookies ("Florentins"), are said to be named after the Italian city of Florence. Originally introduced to France in the sixteenth century by the master chef to Anne, Duchess of Brittany, today, although many regional variations exist, Florentines are considered a specialty of Brittany.

New York City
Sunset Supper à la Française

As the evening sun pours its soft light onto the dining table in this home, high up over the ever-changing lights of Manhattan, the white ceramic geometric plates define the space and the dishes come to life in a joyful contrast of color and textures.

Looking out to Central Park and the Manhattan cityscape, teeming with activity and climbing ever further toward the sky, one might think that this city of constant change and cultural cacophony dismisses history with a casual wave. In truth, New York is more of an amalgamator, a melting pot of cultural and artistic influences, where each home is the unique vessel that carries the memory of past mores and of generations.

To celebrate and reaffirm this very quality, the table is set in the manner known as "le service à la française"—a practice that has its origin in Europe in the Middle Ages and that consisted of presenting all the various dishes at the same time. The effect that was sought was a rich visual feast, where the lightest and the heaviest of courses shared the table of the prepared banquet equally.

The guests served themselves while standing, in the manner of their choosing—a custom that additionally offered them a visual vantage point to enjoy the aesthetic effect of the final display. The plates arranged "à la française" should be laid out along the length of the table, in a symmetrical pattern. Furthermore, the table should not be decorated with any other items, allowing the food to be the decoration.

It wasn't until the nineteenth century that service "à la française" was replaced by service "à la russe." In the now widely adopted and familiar Russian dining style, dishes are brought out sequentially and prepared in a manner so that each diner can help himself or herself.

But on this occasion, in the blink of an eye, we can playfully reconnect to centuries of this French culinary tradition and its storied hostesses.

The simplicity of the table setting, inspired by the modern décor of this apartment, guides the eye toward the sculptures arranged in front of the windows. The vast cityscape sets the mood, while the bronze figures bring the visual focus back to the clean design and the elegant geometry of the dining table and its chairs.

The Taittinger champagne is cooling next to the elegant flutes, the iconic glass design that was expressly engineered for champagne. The stem allows one to hold the glass without affecting the temperature and the narrow mouth prevents the quick loss of carbonation.

Greek Salad

Serves 8

Ingredients

14 ounces (400 g) mixed heirloom tomatoes
1 cucumber
1 green bell pepper
1 medium red onion
1 2/3 cups (300 g) Kalamata or other black olives, pitted
Salt and pepper
3 tablespoons extra virgin olive oil
1 tablespoon red wine vinegar
10 ounces (300 g) feta cheese cut into 1/2-inch
(1 cm) cubes

Preparation

Cut the tomatoes into wedges or large chunks. Cut the cucumber into slices 1/4 inch (5 mm) thick. Thinly slice the bell pepper into rings. Cut the red onion in half and thinly slice.

Place the vegetables in a large salad bowl. Add the olives. Season with salt and pepper, and dress with olive oil and red wine vinegar. Gently toss and add the feta cubes on top and serve.

The colorful raw vegetables and briny Kalamata olives in the Greek salad provide the perfect
balance to the dry texture and pungent taste of feta cheese. The red is the mildest and sweetest
of onion varieties, and is thus the one usually used in salads and other raw dishes.

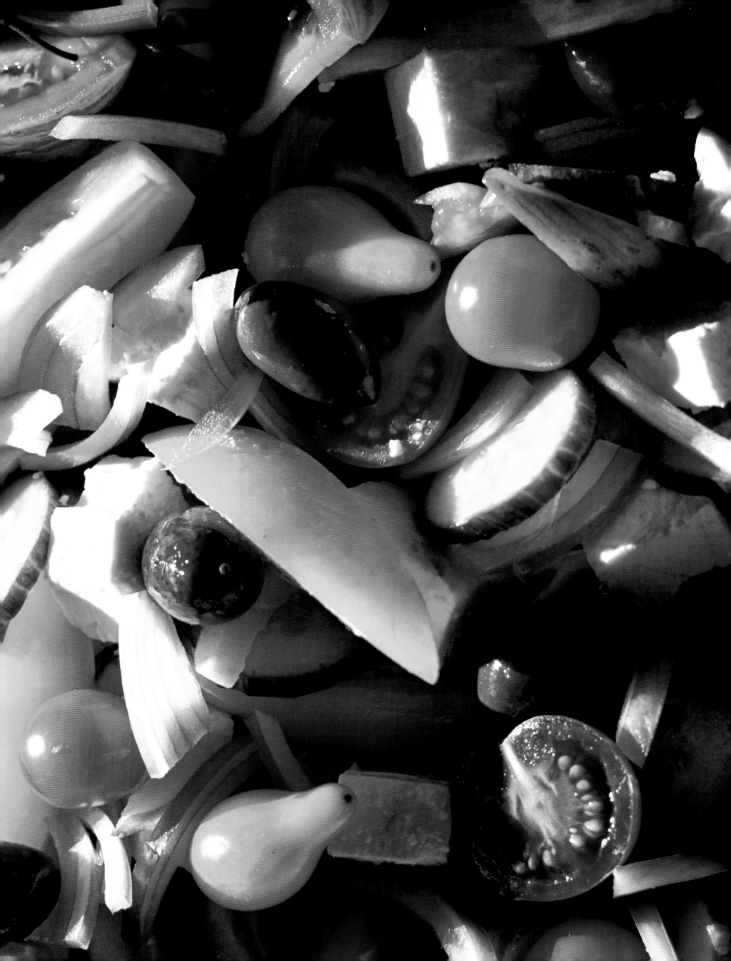

A Lenox Hill Manse

From Louis IX to New Angoulême

In this lovely home located in the Lenox Hill neighborhood of Manhattan, the bust of Saint Louis, king of France, displayed on a stone pedestal at the very center of the dining room, is a moving tribute to Louis IX, the beloved French king, and to his enduring legacy.

During the thirteenth century, the so-called "golden century of Saint Louis," the kingdom of France was at its height in Europe, both politically and economically. The sunlight streaming through the twin patio doors that open to a lovely terrace enhances the serene mood that his figure inspires, but also lends a surprising country feel to this city retreat.

The sculpture of the French king in this New York home is also a heartfelt testament to the longstanding amity that exists between these two nations. That relationship was founded on a shared love of freedom, and the French were America's great friend during their eighteenth-century War of Independence.

Centuries earlier, Louis IX also championed ideals of justice as he created the first-ever court of appeals, where anyone could go and seek the amendment of a judgment. He also introduced the presumption of innocence in criminal procedures. For this reason, Saint Louis can be found portrayed as a standing figure on the roof of the New York State Appellate Court and in the courtroom of the Supreme Court of the United States.

In the sixteenth century, the French were among the first Europeans to reach, and to settle in, New York State. In 1524, long before the Dutch established their colony, Giovanni da Verrazzano, aboard La Dauphine, explored the Hudson River for François I, king of France.

The navigator gave the location that New York City occupies today its first name: *Nouvelle Angoulême* or New Angoulême. The name was chosen to honor his patron, who had been the Count of Angoulême up to his coronation. Standing at the ready, beneath the crowned head of a king, the throne-like copper klismos chairs and the elaborate ormolu candelabras lend the scene a surreal illusion of attending a meal in another era, a forgotten time in a French aristocrat's country manse.

Finally, the table's color palette, highlighted by gold, copper, and vermeil, offers an elegant and subdued color contrast to the burnt ochre tablecloth and aubergine table decorations, allowing the delicate chinaware to fully focus the guests' attention.

The summer light is echoed in golden notes of the table décor for an early supper or "evening meal" among friends. The term *supper* comes from the Old French word *souper* and signifies last meal of the day; whereas the word *dinner* derives from the Latin word meaning "to break one's fast" and refers to the main meal of the day.

Opposite There are many varieties of eggplants, or aubergines. They range from round to oblong, from striped to uniformly colored, and from deep purple to white. Here, a cluster of Italian ceramic eggplants with their slightly smaller deep purple and rounded shapes create a whimsical counterpoint to the formal dinner table setting. *Above* The gold decorative charger plate is chosen in this table setting to complement and highlight the whimsical curves of the border of the dinnerware. Per established etiquette, it can be left on the table throughout the course of the meal.

Black Cod in Miso Sauce

Serves 6

Ingredients

2/3 cup (150 ml) sake
2/3 cup (150 ml) mirin
1/4 cup (50 ml) yuzu juice
15 ounces (450 g) white miso paste
1 cup (225 g) superfine (caster) sugar
6 (7-ounce/200-g) cod fillets
4 stalks lemongrass, for serving
Cooked bok choy, for serving

Preparation

In a saucepan, combine the sake, mirin, and yuzu juice, and bring to a boil.
Boil for 20 seconds to evaporate the alcohol. Reduce the heat to low and add the white miso paste, mixing with a wooden spoon.
When the miso is completely dissolved, increase the heat to high and add the superfine sugar, mixing constantly with the wooden spoon to prevent the contents of the pan from sticking. Once the sugar is completely dissolved, remove the pan from the heat and allow to cool to room temperature.
Blot the cod fillets with paper towels. Place the fillets in a dish and brush them on each side with some of the miso sauce (put about 1/2 cup in a separate bowl before brushing and reserve in the refrigerator). Cover the dish with plastic wrap (cling film) and let it marinate in the refrigerator for 24 hours.
Preheat the oven to 400°F (200°C). Remove the fillets from the miso marinade and set them on a baking sheet. Cook for 10 to 15 minutes. Gently heat the reserved sauce.
Serve the cod with cooked bok choy and garnish with lemongrass stalks. Drizzle the warm sauce over the cod.

Bok choy, a member of the cabbage family, has a number of different names, including pak choi, horse's ear, Chinese celery cabbage, and white mustard cabbage. This graceful vegetable of Chinese origin is available year-round, and its delicate mustardy flavor provides a perfect accompaniment to meat and fish dishes.

Below the Andes

Where Provence Is in the Air

"The king of Provence is the olive tree, the essential element to Provençal cuisine. There is no good cuisine without good oil and there is no Provençal cuisine without garlic." So said Jean-Noël Escudier in his 1964 cookbook *La véritable cuisine provençale et niçoise* (English publication title: *The Wonderful Food of Provence*) that includes some six hundred authentic recipes from Provence.

Comfortably perched on a gentle rolling hill of the Coastal Range, the scenic terrace of this seaside home in Zapallar, Chile, overlooks the low mountains that descend to the Pacific, revealing a landscape blessed by a temperate climate very similar to the French Mediterranean coast. A backdrop that seems designed to explore the Provençal flavor palette highlighted with locally sourced olive oil, fresh vegetables, sweet peppers, and seafood.

Lying between two mountain ranges, the nearby Central Valley is a vast stretch of fertile land home to countless farms that grow vegetables and fruits, including avocados, olives, oranges, tangerines, peaches, walnuts, and the splendid bell peppers that are native to Central and South America—all produce that lends itself to indulging in the French gastronomy that originates in the Provence-Alpes-Côte d'Azur.

Provençal cooking is defined by the use of goat's milk instead of cow dairy products, olive oil and olives rather than butter, seafood and fresh vegetables, as well as an abundance of garlic and other spices.

In 1935, the poet and author Calixtine Chanot-Bullier penned a seminal cookbook on Provençal cuisine, written in the regional Occitan dialect commonly known as langue d'Oc; it distinguishes four distinct culinary traditions in the cuisine that originates in Provence.

The first sub-genre, known as Marseillaise, is famous for fish and fish stews, such as bouillabaisse, as well as meat dishes such as daube; the second Arlesienne and Camarguaise places vegetables above all; the third Toulonnaise and Varoise favors shellfish, eaten raw or cooked in fancy sauces; and finally, the fourth, Niçoise uses different pastas in its recipes as Nice only became part of France in 1860.

Here, far from France's Pays d'Oc, the scent of grilled octopus and bell peppers with garlic transports us, in the blink of an eye, from the slopes of Chile's Coastal Mountain Range and the blue Pacific Ocean to Provence's Esterel Massif and the Côte d'Azur. Pure magic!

The olive tree groves surrounding this cliff-side terrace provide a natural connection to the earth.

A Turkish couscous salad, a zucchini and red onion salad, as well as
avocado, sliced radishes, and celery, complete this summertime menu.

Octopus Salad
Serves 8

Ingredients

2 1/4 cups (550 ml) white wine vinegar, or 2 cups (500 ml) white wine vinegar plus 1/4 cup (50 ml) lemon juice
1/2 (110 g) cup coarse sea salt
4 bay leaves
2 1/4 pounds (1 kg) fresh octopus (or frozen)
5 tablespoons olive oil
2 cloves garlic, crushed
1 teaspoon dried oregano
Salt and pepper
4 boiled potatoes, cut into cubes; see Note
5 celery stalks, peeled and sliced
Chopped fresh parsley
Chopped fresh oregano, for garnish (optional)

Preparation

Fill a large pot with water and add 2 cups (500 ml) vinegar, salt, and bay leaves. Bring to a boil over high heat. Add the octopus and cook over medium-low heat for 30 minutes. Drain the octopus and set aside. When cool enough to handle, cut into pieces (the size is your preference). In a large bowl, combine the olive oil, remaining vinegar or lemon juice, garlic, oregano, and salt and pepper. Add the octopus and mix well. Cover with plastic wrap (cling film) and marinate in the refrigerator overnight (at least 8 hours). When ready to serve, add the boiled potatoes, the celery, and the parsley and gently toss the ingredients. Garnish with additional fresh parsley or oregano.

Note: You can replace the potatoes with green peppers and cucumbers.

The potato, farmed widely in the area covering Peru and Chile, dates as far back as 500 BC, when the Incas cultivated it in the Andes. Brought to Europe in the mid-1500s, the tuber paired with the octopus is a favorite of Italian cooks and found in most Mediterranean cuisines.

94

Above A traditional Greek salad is a wonderful dish to serve any time of the year, but it is particularly suited to dining alfresco.
Opposite The vegetarian eggplant terrine is served here with roasted peppers, a Chilean tomato salsa, garlic cloves, and coarse salt. The red and yellow sweet peppers that accompany the terrine are distinguished by their longer shape and are native to Mexico, Central America, and northern South America.

Eggplant Terrine
Serves 8

Ingredients

6 medium eggplants
1 tablespoon olive oil
4 shallots, finely chopped
3 cloves garlic, crushed
Leaves of 1 bunch fresh basil, chopped,
plus whole leaves for garnish
1/2 cup (45 g) breadcrumbs
1/2 cup (40 g) grated Parmesan
4 eggs, beaten
Salt and pepper
1 teaspoon butter, for the mold
1 tablespoon flour, for the mold
Roasted bell peppers and chopped
tomatoes, for serving; see Note

Preparation

Place the eggplants on a baking sheet lined with parchment paper. Cook for 45 to 60 minutes, until browned (turn them over after 30 minutes); keep the oven on. When they are cool enough to handle, remove the skin and chop the flesh. Heat the oil in a large sauté pan and cook the shallots and garlic, stirring often. When the garlic is fragrant, add the chopped eggplant to the pan. Stir and cook for about 5 minutes.

Transfer the eggplant mixture to a large bowl, along with the chopped basil, breadcrumbs, grated Parmesan, and the beaten eggs. Mix to combine and season with salt and pepper.

Butter and flour a nonstick bread or terrine mold. Transfer the eggplant mixture to the mold and bake in the oven for 35 minutes. Let it cool and remove from mold.

Garnish with reserved basil, slice, and serve with roasted peppers and tomatoes.

Note: When you cook the eggplants, you can also cook a couple of red and yellow peppers. Remove the skins and seeds of the peppers, cut into strips, and season with salt, olive oil, and garlic. These can be served with the eggplant terrine in addition to or in place of the tomatoes.

This eggplant vegetable terrine is a wonderful dish as it is both light and full of flavor. It can be prepared in advance so it is a perfect choice for a garden party or for a winter buffet.

Lunch at the Conservatory

Celebrating Springtime

New York is a strange and wonderful place where, in the blink of an eye and with a careful selection of decorative objects, one can be transported from a noisy modern metropolis to a quiet Eastern-inspired conservatory.

In this whimsical and elegant setting, porcelain parrots and monkeys, wild orchids, and colorful Oriental accents enliven the dining table dressed in linen, and remind us of long-forgotten summer afternoons of childhood—a time when the hours seemed to languish, not to race.

The nature motif extends the soft palette with tones of sand for the tablecloth and coral for the napkins. The floral accents of the table are echoed in the unusual green water tumblers.

A water glass, or tumbler, set out on the dining table is an every-day feature on any table prepared for a meal. It is hard to imagine this simplest of customs was not always so readily accepted.

During the reign of Louis XIV, when the dining etiquette had reached its greatest complexity, no drinking glasses were set on the dining table. When any guest, including the king, felt thirsty, he or she would discreetly ask for a drink from a servant who presented the drink on a tray. Once the person had emptied the glass it was immediately handed back to the servant, never touching the table.

Glassware and its selection is a central element to the tone of the gathering and underscores the nature of the meal. The myriad shapes, materials, and decorative styles of glassware—ranging from bubble glass to inlaid china, from gilded crystal flutes to bohemian cut-glass goblets—offer an immense range of possibilities, freeing the imagination to assemble and choose to one's delight.

Here the glasses set the tone of grace and refinement as they disperse the rays of sunlight on this late-spring day, offering the opportunity to open a window into a slower time when lunch with friends could be transformed into a lingering afternoon spent in conversation.

The beige linen tablecloth provides a delicate canvas that highlights the china laid out along the length of the dining table.

Opposite A centerpiece that includes two delicate white porcelain crested parakeets enhances the floral and wildlife mood evoked at the dining table. *Above* The gold, wine, and ochre colors evident in the floral pattern on the Royal Crown Derby starter plate are also present in the leaf pattern of the classic Mottahedeh Nelson Rockefeller Collection dinner plate.

Roast Loin of Pork with Mustard & Sage

Serves 8

Ingredients

1 (3-pound or 1 1/2-kg) loin of pork
1 cup (232 g) crème fraîche
1 tablespoon whole grain mustard
2 teaspons Dijon mustard
1/2 cup chopped fresh sage leaves, plus whole leaves
fresh and fried, for garnish
1 head garlic, cloves separated and peeled
Salt and pepper
Roasted Romanesco and caramelized sweet potatoes,
for serving

Preparation

Preheat the oven to 350°F (180°C). Place the pork loin
in a baking dish.
In a medium bowl, mix the crème fraîche, mustards, and
chopped sage. Cover the top and sides of the loin with this
mixture. Arrange the garlic cloves around the pork loin.
Pour a glass of water into the bottom of the dish.
Bake for 1 hour, until cooked through. Transfer the cooked
pork loin to a cutting board.
Pour a glass of hot water into the baking dish to deglaze,
using a wooden spoon to release the bits at the bottom of
the dish. Season with salt and pepper.
Slice the pork loin and place on a serving platter. Drizzle
with some of the sauce, serving the rest in a bowl alongside,
and garnish with fresh and fried sage leaves.
Serve with roasted Romanesco and caramelized
sweet potatoes.

*Note: This dish can also be served with roasted Brussels sprouts
or broccoli or caramelized carrots in addition to or in place of the
Romanesco and sweet potatoes.*

The lively colors of the caramelized sweet potatoes and the Romanesco Italian cauliflower are the perfect
complement to the subtle earthy tones and milder flavors of the sage and the meat. The sage, both
fresh and fried, at the center of the plated pork loin roast provides a burst of flavor and aroma
that does not overpower but rather enhances the subtle nuances of the meat.

A Country Feast

Harvesting Stars

It seems as though one could choose to dine in any corner of this wonderful country home in Normandy's apple country and be rewarded for one's whimsy: the air fragrant with the aroma of ripening apples and the sunlight of Northern France awakening impossible shades of green.

Actually, the modern dining room is a rather new custom that in Europe only dates back to the seventeenth century. Its ancient ancestor has its roots with the Romans and their use of the *triclinium*, a way of sharing a meal that was adopted by the Gauls in the first century. It was customary for the homes of the well-to-do to possess a winter, a summer, and an outdoor triclinium. This dining setup consisted of three lounge beds placed around the table, where the male diners would recline while the women and children sat on chairs.

In France, during the Middle Ages, whether the event involved a communal banquet or an intimate dinner, meals were served anywhere that struck one's fancy; be it in a courtyard, the bedroom, the library, the antechamber, the garden, or a gallery. No matter the location, a table was purposely erected by placing a wooden top on two trestles that were then covered in a tablecloth and a long runner, which was placed close to the diners so that they could wipe their hands, their faces, and even the cutlery!

It was only in the eighteenth century, with the growing popularity of a more refined and regimented dining etiquette in France, that this changed; dining rooms began to appear regularly as an architectural feature in new homes, while in other instances, existing rooms of the château were converted to this function, where no dining room had been planned.
So be it! Dining where we please, in the old way. Lunch will take place in the secluded shelter provided by the half-timbered farmhouse, beneath the age-old beams of its outdoor roof.

Later we shall sup under the branches of the apple trees that lend an aura of intimate romance to this secret garden, and indulge in the perfect dish of moules marinière under the stars.

Opposite The pale blue rattan chairs, the dark green balloton Venetian glasses, and the naturalistic designs of the tablecloth present a fresh color palette and an eclectic mix of cultural influences. *Following pages* The fruits displayed in the centerpiece and the windowsill are a beautiful reminder of the rich history that apples have in this corner of France.

Green Puy Lentil Salad
Serves 8

Ingredients

2 cups (400 g) green Puy lentils
Salt
2 bay leaves
1 carrot, cut into 3 to 4 pieces
1 clove garlic, peeled
2 tablespoons red wine vinegar or lemon juice
2 teaspoons Dijon mustard
2 tablespoons hazelnut oil
2 tablespoons grapeseed or vegetable oil
Pepper
2 shallots, finely chopped
2 tablespoons chopped parsley
Parsley or chervil leaves, for serving

Preparation

Rinse the lentils and place in a saucepan with 6 cups (1 1/2 liters) of cold water, salt, the bay leaves, the carrot, and the garlic. Simmer until tender but still firm in the center, about 25 minutes.
Remove and discard bay leaves, garlic, and carrot pieces. Drain the lentils, rinse with cold water, and refrigerate. When you are ready to serve the salad, whisk the vinegar, mustard, and oils to make a vinaigrette. Season with salt and pepper.
Transfer the chilled lentils to a bowl. Toss with the vinaigrette. Add the shallots and parsley and toss again. Garnish with parsley or chervil.

Note: This salad is also lovely with tiny cubes of green apple, fennel, or celery folded into the mix.

The joyful Zulu plate chargers and the riot of color and shapes of the tableware make the tonal contrast between the dark colors of the legumes and the bright shrimp, lemons, and carrots even more enticing.

110

Above The cutlery and chinaware in this setting include a delicately painted wide rimmed soup bowl, as well as a fish knife and soup spoon. The course to come is a dish of mussels in their own delicious broth. Plenty of crusty bread is served alongside. *Opposite* The casual and festive quality of alfresco (or outdoor) dining is especially popular in the summer months in Normandy. The climate is just right to put the guests in a celebratory mood and entice them to enjoy the magical atmosphere of the garden in the evening.

Musical Chairs & Gentlemen's Hats

A Mystery Is Solved

Our world has embraced the idea of a lifestyle where dining rooms are no longer de rigueur. To wit, in this Upper East Side apartment in Manhattan, a set of deliberately mismatched chairs is at the heart of the mood of this creative working lunch—and its dining area has been incorporated into the sitting room.

Nowadays, this is not an unusual layout, and in the case of even more bohemian lifestyles, a loft-like living space or great room often accommodates a kitchen, a dining area, and a conversation corner. It is hard to imagine that there was a time in France when such an approach would have been unthinkable, and all manner of human interactions were governed by the strictest of etiquettes, at the dining table and elsewhere; all leading up to the king himself.

When the table was set for the king, only his chair was put in place. Folding stools were arranged at the ends of the table for other dinner guests, those of the highest social rank. All other attendees stood in front and watched! As far as dress is concerned, it gets even more complicated as French court etiquette demanded that gentlemen would remove their hats in presence of the king, who alone wore a hat. However, at dinner, all gentlemen wore a hat apart from the king. When such a person was addressed by the king he would respond by first removing his hat!

Today, unless dealing with a strictly formal occasion, seating etiquette only requires that the guest of honor is seated to the right of the host, while other guests are seated, for effect or out of respect for traditions, as the host believes is best.

In fact, seated or standing, à la Française or à la Russe, wine or whiskey, stem glasses or tumblers, new decorative candles or spent and unlit, tablecloths or placemats... the preferences of the individual host or hostess are acceptable, in almost all aspects of dining; indeed these choices are a declaration of savoir-vivre and savoir-faire.

It seems that the gourmand Brillat-Savarin was the most prescient about our modern aspirations when entertaining at home: "To receive guests is to take charge of their happiness during the entire time they are under your roof."

Lace and tangerines, a Russian dish reinvented by the French, an eclectic mix of art and furnishings; these are the elements that set a mood where anything can happen...

Above The Meissen Yellow Dragon dinnerware features a scalloped rim and is highlighted by a border made of two long yellow and brown stylized dragons with touches of gold. The Salmon Coulibiac is a perfect choice if you are planning to entertain, as it can be made well in advance. *Opposite* Grilled endives and russet potatoes offer a wonderful combination of textures and flavors. It was Antoine-Augustin Parmentier who popularized the potato, in 1779, in his *Manière de faire le pain de pommes de terre*, which described how to make potato bread. Up until then, the French had considered the potato to be animal feed.

Salmon Coulibiac

Serves 6

Ingredients

1 pound (500 g) salmon fillet, with skin
5 cups (1 1/4 liters) boiling water
1 1/4 cups (250 g) round, short-grain rice
5 eggs
5 1/4 ounces (150 g) spinach
1 tablespoons (15 g) butter
Salt and pepper
1 sheet puff pastry, thawed
1/2 lemon
Chopped dill, for serving

Preparation

Wrap the salmon in plastic wrap (cling film). Place the salmon in a pot with the boiling water. Poach the salmon for 5 minutes over medium heat; the salmon will not be fully cooked. Drain. When cool enough to handle, remove the skin.
Boil the rice for 15 minutes. Hard-boil 4 of the eggs for 10 minutes, then peel them.
In a frying pan, sweat the spinach in the butter. Season with salt and pepper.
Spread the puff pastry sheet over plastic wrap (cling film) and form a large rectangle (8 x 16 inches/20 x 40 cm). Cover the dough with the spinach leaves, leaving a 1-inch (2 1/2-cm) border.
On top of the spinach, spread a thin layer of the rice, then lay the salmon in the middle with the hard-boiled eggs cut in 2. Fold both long sides of the dough to cover the fish and eggs. Then press the sides of the rectangle together to seal the dough. Cut off excess dough. Crimp or roll the long sides decoratively and brush with water to seal.
Cover tightly with plastic wrap (cling film), and allow to rest for 30 minutes in the refrigerator. Preheat the oven to 400°F (200°C).
Remove the plastic and slash the top in multiple places, then make 3 vents in the pastry. Brush with egg wash.
Bake in the oven for 30 minutes: 15 minutes at 400°F/200°C and then 15 minutes at 350°F/180°C.

Lemon Dill Sauce

Makes 2 cups

Ingredients

1 stick plus 2 tablespoons (150 g) butter
1/2 cup (100 ml) heavy cream
Juice of 1 lemon
1 bunch dill, chopped
Salt and pepper

Preparation

In a saucepan, melt 2 tablespoons of the butter and add the cream. Simmer until the cream is warm. Whisk in the lemon juice and dill and season with salt. Add the remaining butter 1 tablespoon at a time, whisking to combine between additions.

Auguste Escoffier, the father of French cooking, included the recipe for Salmon Coulibiac in his cookbook *Le Guide Culinaire*. It is said that he developed the recipe, based on the traditional Russian *kulebiaka*, while working at his uncle's restaurant in Nice, France.

East Hampton
A Tale of Land and Sea

This East Hampton home reflects the area's cultural roots with an elegant mix of English and early-American furniture and objects. On the table, the elements presented continue this interplay of cultural influences with the goal of creating a harmonious and yet surprising table setting.

Arriving in 1648, long before the French lent a hand to the rebellious colonists to ensure their independence, the English farmers, fishermen, and their families came across Long Island Sound and founded East Hampton. They came in search of a way to make a living from the land and the sea.

For over three hundred years, the fertile soil, moderate weather, ample sunshine, and fresh, clean water of this splendid region afforded the original inhabitants and generations of new immigrants the opportunity to prosper, and later to develop their very own farm-grown specialty crops.

In this home, the town's proximity to the ocean is celebrated by the large grouping of staghorn coral, benitier shell, starfish, conches, and fox seashells that are displayed on the sideboard. Its farm credentials are reflected in the center-piece featuring colorful produce of the farms that still surround the village.

The rich soil and the distance to New York enabled East Hampton to remain a fairly quiet rural farm community until the early decades of the twentieth century. That was the time when many wealthy, and some quite famous, summer visitors built their leisure homes along the coastline, among them the parents of Jacqueline Bouvier Kennedy.

In the postwar years, artists, writers, and other city dwellers in search of a quieter life began to migrate farther east and made their year-round homes toward the end of Long Island; the rhythms of life changed once again as the newcomers stayed to enjoy the offerings of all the seasons.

The Northeast fall foliage colors that greet residents after the summer crowds have gone are beautifully re-created in the plum linen table covering, red linen napkins, and cauli-flowers of this visually striking natural tableau.

The purple and orange theme of the table linens is an extension
of the colors used in the floral and vegetable centerpiece.

Above The introduction of cutlery designed for various food types, such as fish cutlery, dates back to the 1850s when an increasingly wealthy middle class elevated dining to a performance intended to impress and to display its wealth. *Opposite* The wildlife theme of the table decorations is echoed in the Richard Ginori dinner plate that is displayed atop a gold charger. The choice of the charger is intended to provide a transitional color between the predominantly white china and the darker hues of the table.

Martine's Lane

Silver Swans in the East End

History is beautifully revealed as the Southampton summer light streams through the windows of the dining room onto the soft contours of the green glass goblets and brings to life the naturalistic shapes of the fanciful dinnerware.

The colonial and English accents of the furnishings point to a time when this village was named after the British Earl of Southampton and, in 1648, became the first permanent English settlement in the state of New York. For well over a century, English customs, as well as religious and political ideas, defined Southampton's identity. It was not until 1783, at the end of the American Revolution that, with the support of the French, the British military finally relinquished its control of Southampton.

The elegant Argand oil lamps displayed on the sideboard are a reminder that Southampton also owes a great debt to the whaling industry, which brought hundreds of millions of dollars to eastern Long Island in the first half of the nineteenth century.

Long before 1859, when oil began to be pumped out of the ground in Pennsylvania, the most sought-after fuel for lamps and other uses was the pure oil found in the heads of sperm whales. Hundreds of whaling vessels sailed the world's oceans in search of whales; and Long Island, Sag Harbor and Greenport became the main whaling ports. Indeed, revenue from whaling operations represented, at its height, one fifth of the American gross domestic product.

The whimsical green cabbage ceramics designed by Raphael Bordallo Pinheiro in the late nineteenth century, and produced in Portugal at the Fábrica de Faianças in Caldas, are a reminder of the refined ambitions and tastes of the Gilded Age: an epoch that gave rise to the new Southampton. It was a time when the steam engine enabled intercontinental voyages and the growth of global trade, and a fresh wave of French political refugees, fleeing the failed 1848 revolution, enjoyed the evermore-sophisticated lifestyle of the American elite.

As the afternoon stretches out into early evening, it is a wonderful room to frame a get-together over an early supper comprised of potage made from locally grown tomatoes and wild brown rice with lobster.

The red walls of the dining room as well as the rural landscape
beyond its walls are the leitmotif of the dinner table decorations.

Preceding pages The elegant workmanship apparent in the nineteenth-century silver swan centerpieces creates a dramatic contrast with the simple machine made geometry of the green Depression glass goblets. This type of glassware was produced in the United States and Canada around the time of the Great Depression. *Above* The cabbage design by Raphael Bordallo Pinheiro is a splendid example of the artistic talent, the craft, and the humor of this seminal nineteenth-century Portuguese humorist and artist.

Tomato & Pepper Soup
Serves 6

Ingredients

3 pounds (1 1/2 kg) small red tomatoes, such as cherry tomatoes, baby plum tomatoes, or San Marzano datterini
2 red bell peppers
3 shallots
2 cloves garlic
1 tablespoon extra-virgin olive oil
2 cups hot vegetable or chicken broth or boiling water
Salt
Sugar, if needed
1 tablespoon (15 g) butter
Dill, for garnish

Preparation

Wash the tomatoes and red peppers then cut them in small pieces.
Peel and chop the shallots and garlic.
In a medium size casserole heat the olive oil and add the shallots and garlic and sauté them until transparent and soft.
Add the chopped peppers.
Continue stirring for 2 minutes, then throw in the tomatoes and cook for another 2 minutes over medium heat. Add the broth and season with salt. Increase the temperature and simmer briskly for 10 minutes. Turn the heat off.
Remove from the heat and set aside to cool for 10 minutes.
With a stick/immersion blender purée until very smooth. Press the mixture through a chinois and discard skin and seeds. Return the soup to the heat in a clean casserole. Taste and adjust seasoning with sugar if necessary. Keep warm.
Before serving, stir in the butter. Garnish with dill.

The texture and color of the tomato potage made from ripened local tomatoes is enhanced by the contrast with the rich greens of the soup bowl.

Lobster Newberg

Serves 6

Ingredients

4 live lobsters
Salt
4 tablespoons (60 g) butter
1 tablespoon all-purpose/plain flour
1 1/4 cups (300 ml) milk
1/4 cup (60 ml) whipping cream
Pepper
1 pinch grated nutmeg
1/2 teaspoon paprika
1/2 teaspoon ground turmeric
1/4 cup (60 ml) Noilly Prat, sherry,
or madeira wine
2 egg yolks
Brown rice and wild rice, or steamed potatoes,
for serving

Preparation

Fill a stockpot or lobster pot 3/4 with water.
Salt generously and bring to a boil.
Add the lobsters. Cover and cook until lobster flesh is firm, about 9 minutes from the time the water returns to a boil.
Remove the lobsters and let them drain and cool.
Shell the lobsters, cutting from tail to head. Chop the flesh into large cubes. Leave the claws whole.
In a large saucepan, melt 2 tablespoons (30 g) butter.
Whisk in the flour. Cook, whisking, over low heat for 1 minute.
Add the milk and cream in a thin stream, whisking constantly. Still whisking, bring the mixture to a boil over medium heat. Continue to cook, still whisking, for 5 minutes. Reach the whisk into the corners of the pan and be sure to scrape the bottom.
Season with salt, pepper, and nutmeg and remove from the heat.
Melt the remaining butter in a large skillet and sauté the lobster. Season with paprika and turmeric.
Deglaze the skillet with the Noilly Prat and cook until the liquid has reduced by half.
If the cream sauce has cooled, gently rewarm. Whisk in the egg yolks until thoroughly combined. Add the lobster to the sauce and toss to coat thoroughly.
If necessary, keep the lobster warm in an oven set to 200°F (100°C).
Serve with a mixture of brown rice and wild rice.

132

Brown rice and wild rice are a wonderful combination of grains. But while brown rice is rice, what we call wild rice is actually a grass. There are four different species of wild rice: three are native to North America and have been grown and harvested by Native Americans for hundreds of years.

All the World's a Stage

The Maunsel House Magic

A weekend in Somerset offers innumerable opportunities to enjoy the local produce and experience one of the most romantic and idiosyncratic corners of England. It is also an occasion to orchestrate a multi-chapter culinary event that combines décor, table settings, and menus in novel ways, for the entertainment of the guests.

A stately home that has been in the Slade family since the thirteenth century, Maunsel House is the perfect setting for staging meals in the garden, on a classic dining table, or in one of the many quirky and formal rooms.

As the guests arrive, the mood is set by planning their first meal in the formal dining room under the watchful gaze of the aristocratic portraits that adorn the walls. The culinary journey begins with a light tuna tartare served on a table adorned by fresh flowers and candlesticks. The absence of a tablecloth suggests that, although elegant and refined, in both setting and menu, the meal is an invitation to enjoy the fragrant English countryside that peeks through the open doors.

The next day a smaller party is treated to a British lunch of lamb and sweet peas served on a formally dressed and elaborately decorated table in a small sitting room. The sought-after effect is to create a contrast between the classic and elegant table décor and the eccentric collection of the 7th Baronet, which includes a suit of armor and an Asian black bear wearing a fez.

Dinner in the beamed pantry is an opportunity to gather around a table decorated to evoke the boisterous atmosphere of a Tudor tavern. Thus, the long, narrow wood table is adorned with simple pewter and silver objects and clear white glasses and carafes, and features the hearty and time-tested dish of duck and mushrooms.

The final act is set in the garden near the covered walkway; it features a table setting inspired by spring and the home's wonderful flower garden. Anchored by the pastel-colored tablecloth, decorated with a large bouquet of fragrant lilies and pink roses, the round table offers a feeling of intimacy in the large, open space.

The Sunday meal of salmon, topped off by the quintessentially French profiteroles for dessert, is a nod to the journey we are about to make as we head back home to France!

A number of family portraits add a historical note to the elaborate décor of the aquamarine and gold Maunsel House dining room. In keeping with this palette, the table is set with chinaware and linens similar in color, as well as aquamarine candles.

136

Above and Opposite The dining table for the ten guests is strewn with white roses cut from the garden, adding a fresh detail to a wonderfully grand and yet surprisingly cozy table. The nobility in late Tudor England usually dined at a similar rectangular-shaped table made of oak. Their dining etiquette dictated that the highest-ranking person sat at the top of the table, similar to our custom today. Here, an Italian Renaissance Savonarola scissor chair is chosen to emphasize the hierarchy of the guests.

Tuna Tartare
Serves 5

Ingredients

14 ounces (400g) bluefin tuna
3 scallions/green onions, green stalks only
1 tablespoon chopped garlic
1 tablespoon chopped shallot
1 tablespoon minced fresh ginger
1 tablespoon black and white sesame seeds
1/2 teaspoon paprika
1 tablespoon sesame oil
Salt and pepper
2 tablespoons lime juice
1 tablespoon soy sauce
Fresh cilantro/coriander leaves, for garnish
Microherbs, for garnish
Pickled ginger, for garnish

Preparation

Cut the tuna into small cubes. Finely chop the scallion/green onion stalks (do not use the bulbs).
Mix the tuna cubes, chopped scallion/green onion stalks, garlic, shallot, ginger, sesame seeds, paprika, and sesame oil. Add salt and freshly ground pepper, mix gently, and refrigerate for a few minutes.
Mix the lime juice and the soy sauce.
When serving, arrange the marinated tuna on serving plates and drizzle a few drops of the sauce on top. Garnish with cilantro/coriander leaves and microherbs. Top with pickled ginger.

The tuna tartare is a light, fresh, and non-meat version of the French beef tartare. Its origin is uncertain, but it owes
its popularity to Shigefumi Tachibe, a Japanese-born, French-trained chef, who reintroduced the dish in 1984.

Rack of Lamb
Serves 4

Ingredients

2 tablespoons olive oil
1 rack of lamb
2 whole heads garlic, halved crosswise
1 tablespoon herbes de Provence
Salt and pepper
Mixed garden peas (sugar snaps, petits pois,
and snow peas), tomatoes Provençal, or cooked
potatoes, for serving

Preparation

Preheat the oven to 450°F (240°C). Coat a baking dish
with olive oil.
Scrape the fat off the rack of lamb with the tip of a knife,
without touching the flesh.
Place the rack of lamb in the prepared baking dish,
fat side up, along with the garlic. Sprinkle with the
herbes de Provence. Season with salt and pepper.
Bake for 5 minutes. Lower the oven temperature
to 400°F (210°C) and cook for another 15 minutes.
At the end of the cooking time, cover the lamb with
a sheet of aluminum foil.
Let rest for 15 minutes, then carve into individual ribs.
Serve immediately with the garden peas.

Preceding pages A suit of armor and an Asian black bear wearing a fez flank a Jacobean carved cupboard in this small sitting room, where lunch
for four will feature the quintessentially French dish of *carré d'agneau du printemps* (rack of spring lamb). *Opposite* Lamb chops are incredibly
delicious and tender. Here, the chops have been Frenched, meaning that the meat has been scraped from the ends of the rib bones.

144

Alberto Pinto's Sous Bois dinner plates echo the woodsy tone of our
country-inspired supper of duck with roasted figs and wild mushrooms.

Duck Breast with Roasted Figs
Serves 6

Ingredients

12 fresh figs
6 duck breasts
3 tablespoons honey
Leaves from 2 sprigs fresh rosemary, chopped
Salt and pepper
Rosti potatoes, for serving

Preparation

Preheat the oven to 400°F (210°C).
Wash, wipe, and split the figs into 2 lengthwise.
Cut shallow slits in the duck breast slightly with a knife.
In a hot frying pan set over medium heat, place the duck breast in the pan skin side down. Allow the fat to melt and the skin to brown for about 3 minutes. Once the skin is well colored, turn the duck breasts over and continue cooking for 2 minutes.
Place the duck and figs in a baking dish. Cover the breasts and figs with honey and sprinkle with rosemary, and salt and pepper. Bake for 7 to 10 minutes depending on the desired degree of doneness.
Transfer the duck to a carving board to rest for 5 minutes covered by a sheet of aluminum foil; reserve the pan juice. Slice the duck into thin slices, ensuring that each slice includes fat and meat.
Divide the sliced duck and figs among serving plates.
Drizzle with the pan juices just before serving with potatoes.

Sautéed Wild Mushrooms
Serves 6

Ingredients

14 ounces (400 g) cèpes or porcini
14 ounces (400 g) chanterelles
14 ounces (400 g) shiitake
14 ounces (400 g) wild mushrooms
6 tablespoons (90g) butter
1 tablespoon olive oil
4 shallots, thinly sliced
2 cloves garlic, crushed
Salt and pepper
Leaves of 1/2 bunch parsley, chopped

Preparation

Clean the mushrooms and slice or chop them. Heat the butter and oil in a large sauté pan over medium heat, then add the shallots and garlic and cook until the shallots are translucent.
Add the mushrooms. Cook for about 3 minutes on high heat, or until there is no more water in the pan. The mushrooms should be nicely browned. Season with salt and pepper. Garnish the cooked mushrooms with chopped parsley and serve immediately.

Preceding page and Opposite The royal commemorative objects and World War I memorabilia in the beamed dining room are an exotic visual feast that blends beautifully with a dish of mixed mushrooms that include cèpes, chanterelles, and shiitake.

Pink roses, a pale pink floral tablecloth, and rosé bring
the beauty of this English garden right onto the table.

Saumon à l'Unilatéral
Serves 4

Ingredients

4 (6- to 8-ounce/170- to 226-g) salmon fillets,
skin on
1 1/2 teaspoons coarse sea salt
1 teaspoon pink peppercorns, crushed,
or fresh chopped dill or dried dill
Celery, radish, and avocado salad with lemon dressing,
or chopped leeks sautéed in butter, for serving

Preparation

Heat a nonstick sauté pan over high heat.
Sprinkle salt and the peppercorns (or dill) on both sides of
the fish. Place the salmon, skin side down, in the hot pan.
Reduce the heat to low. Cover and cook for 2 to 3 minutes,
until the salmon is slightly translucent on top. (The cooking
time varies according to the size of the fillets.)
Serve with celery, radish, and avocado salad with lemon
dressing, or chopped leeks sautéed in butter.

The pink peppercorns, sliced green avocados, bright yellow lemons, red and white split radishes, and pale green celery are the perfect complement
to the salmon's iconic color. When it comes to choosing the sour note, given that limes are slightly more bitter than lemons, one may be better
than the other depending on the dish. With this salmon, both lemons and limes make excellent additions to the fish's flavor profile.

Summertime Delights

East Egg & the French Riviera

The new season on the East End of Long Island begins with the large crystal chandelier exercising its kaleidoscopic magic over the glistening table, which is adorned in French china and glassware in shades of blue and aquamarine.

After the Long Island Railroad was consolidated in 1876, the East End's community of summer residents expanded significantly, and the changes that took place in this bucolic corner of the Eastern seaboard were as rapid as they were dramatic. Within just a few years, Southampton would grow into the place to be and be seen.

As early as 1893, the area was described in the *New York Times* as follows: "The beautiful villages clustering around old Southampton, including Quogue, Good Ground, the rest of the Hamptons, and the incomparable Shinnecock Hills, combine to make as close an approach to Eden as can be found in a long journey. Exclusive, in the best sense of the word, society is here represented during the summer by its choicest spirits."

Soon enough, the over-the-top lifestyle of the East End paralleled that of New York in the Roaring Twenties. The characters, the mansions, the endless summertime parties, and the display of wealth that animated this community are portrayed in detail in F. Scott Fitzgerald's *The Great Gatsby*.

Fitzgerald wrote his seminal novel while residing in Valescure, France, a small town on the French Riviera between Monaco and Marseille. Even after he was published in the United States, success came slowly, so he returned to Paris. There Fitzgerald would spend nights drinking with his friend Ernest Hemingway at the Dingo American Bar and Restaurant in Montmartre, a notorious all-night haunt.

Summer is the engine in the life of the Riviera, as it was in East Egg. As Nick Caraway, Gatsby's confidant, observes: "And so with the sunshine and the great bursts of leaves growing on the trees, just as things grow in fast movies, I had that familiar conviction that life was beginning over again with the summer."

In this airy and elegant home, the summer days and the summer dinners will be made to linger as long as possible—for as long as there is a warm evening breeze on the veranda and for as long as the flowers for the centerpieces still bloom in the garden.

A riot of summertime colors set against the dark wood of the dining table creates a sense of joy for this family gathering.

154

Above The hand-blown wine goblets in a stunning aqua color create a visual connection to both the linen placemats and the hydrangeas from the garden. *Opposite* The delicate stem of the blue cornflower serves as a visual guide to bring the eye from the Villeroy and Bosch Flora salad plate to the geometric pattern of the Mottahedeh blue and white dinner plate.

Boeuf en Gelée
Serves 8

Ingredients

2 1/4 pounds (1 kg) beef (spare rib, beef chuck,
or scotch beef)
1 veal foot
1 bouquet garni
6 carrots, peeled and sliced
2 cloves garlic
1 large onion, studded with a clove and cut into quarters
1 red bell pepper, seeded and chopped into large pieces
1 teaspoon coriander seeds
1 tablespoon coarse sea salt
10 peppercorns
2 tablespoons unsalted butter or vegetable oil
Salt and pepper
Leaves of 1 bunch parsley
4 sheets gelatin, softened in cold water and drained
4 spring onions or scallions, chopped
Potato salad and string bean salad, for serving

Preparation

Place the beef and the veal foot in a large pot or Dutch oven.
Cover with cold water.
Bring to the boil and remove the foam that rises to the top.
Do this for 5 minutes.
Add the bouquet garni, half of the carrots, the garlic, the
onion with the clove, the red pepper, the coriander, the coarse
salt, and the peppercorns. Cover and let cook, over low heat
for 2 1/2 to 3 hours, until the meat is tender.
In a medium saucepan over medium heat, cook the remaining
carrots with 2 inches (5 cm) of water, the butter, and salt.
Remove the meat from the pot, trim the fat, and cut into
slices. Discard the vegetables and the veal foot.
Season the cooking liquid with salt and pepper, if necessary.
Place several parsley leaves in the bottom of the terrine,
then fill the terrine with the slices of meat. Alternate slices
of meat with a few carrot slices. Filter the broth, then mix in
4 softened gelatin leaves and whisk until dissolved. Pour the
broth in, and top with fresh chopped spring onions and the
remaining parsley leaves. Let cool, covered, in the refrigerator
for 8 hours.

*Note: Serve with a dressing made with French Dijon mustard, vinegar,
salt and pepper, chopped hard-boiled eggs, chopped parsley, a few capers,
and olive oil. Accompany the dish with potato salad and string bean salad.*

Aspic is a dish in which ingredients are set into a gelatin made from a meat stock.
Antonin Carême devoted himself to refining the art of preparing foods *en gelée*.

Above The blue-and-white-themed dining table set on the veranda provides a sense of timeless elegance and summer days. *Opposite* The dessert, originally called a "Napolitain," is a sweet treat in the style of Naples. It is known in France as mille-feuille ("thousand leaves") for its many flaky layers of pastry surrounding its custard cream. The great French chef and pastry artist Antonin Carême was the first to popularize the dessert in the early 1800s, but even then he described it as being "of ancient origin."

Normandy

The Potteries & "Les Treis Cats"

The product of the area known as The Potteries, the romantic printed plates that are displayed on the dining table are not only a testament to English ingenuity in the 1750s, but also proof that the English are still very much a presence in Normandy.

Indeed, deep in the countryside of Normandy, at a dinner table set near the fireplace, one can still glean the important heritage left by the centuries of English presence. From the Tudor architecture that seamlessly blends with later French stylistic evolutions, the Staffordshire plates displayed on the dining table, and the moving monuments of war left in the more recent past, the presence of the English is felt in Normandy as nowhere else in France.

It was only after countless diplomatic and military maneuvers and reversals lasting centuries that the English House of Anjou finally surrendered the Duchy of Normandy to the French monarchs. This happened after the death of Richard I of England, better known as Richard Cœur de Lion (Richard the Lionheart), who among his titles was also Duke of Normandy and spent the vast majority of his reign and adult life living in France, where his tomb can be found.

Despite this surrender, fifty years would pass before the English throne formally recognized the French claim. Two hundred years later, the English re-conquered Normandy during the Hundred Years War. It was only in 1450 that the French finally achieved permanent control of the region.

Nowhere is the blending of these two important cultural heritages better illustrated than in the region's coat of arms. Normandy is represented by an image of two or three lions rampant (also referred to as leopards, depending on heraldic tradition) on a red shield. In the Norman language, the heraldic depiction of the three figures is "Les Treis Cats" (the three cats), while the emblem with two figures is nicknamed "Les P'tits Cats" (the little cats)!

The charm of country life is mirrored in the rural illustrations that adorn the Staffordshire plates. The distinctive blue of the English transferware is echoed in the joyous colors of the centerpiece, made up of Normandy's wildflowers and a plaster sculpture of a boar. It is a celebration and a salute to the peaceful resolution of these shared histories.

The centerpiece, featuring a porcelain sculpture of a wild boar surrounded by blue flowers, is a reminder that the hunting of wild boar remains very popular both in Normandy and in many other parts of France.

A wonderful example of Josiah Spode's innovative 1770 transfer-printing technique that became enormously
popular in England in the nineteenth century. The manufacture of this plate is credited to Copeland Spode
after William Copeland and Thomas Garrett purchased the firm in 1833.

Sole Meunière
Serves 8

Ingredients

4 whole soles, gutted, scaled, and skinned
8 medium yellow potatoes
2 tablepoons (10 g) coarse sea salt
1 tablespoon all-purpose/plain flour
1 tablespoon vegetable oil
Juice of 1 lemon
4 tablespoons (60 g) butter
Salt and pepper
1 tablespoon chopped parsley
Lemon quarters and blanched samphire,
for serving

Preparation

Rinse and dry the fish.
Peel the potatoes and trim them so they are barrel-
shaped and all the same size. Fill a saucepan with
4 cups (1 liter) water and add the coarse sea salt and
the potatoes. Bring to a boil and cook until potatoes
are tender, about 17 minutes. Drain and keep warm.
Spread the flour on a large plate and dredge the
fish in the flour. Shake off any excess.
Place the vegetable oil in a large skillet over high heat.
Brown the fish on one side, then turn and cook for 2
additional minutes.
Turn the heat to low and add the lemon juice
and the butter.
Cook for 1 additional minute. Season with salt
and pepper and sprinkle with parsley.
Baste the fish with the sauce from the pan.
Arrange the fish on a serving dish with the lemon
quarters. Drizzle any sauce remaining in the pan
over the fish. Serve with the potatoes.

163

Dover sole is a mainstay of the European table that can be found in the shallow waters from the Mediterranean
to the North Sea. The name "Dover" was tacked onto this fish because the English town of Dover supplied more
fish to London's Billingsgate Fish Market than any other fishing village. Samphire, also known as sea asparagus,
grows in the rocky areas near the North Atlantic coast of France. It is a perfect accompaniment to fish.

On the Côte Fleurie

Dining by the Sea

As the afternoon light softens the contours of the room and, in the distance, the sun glistens on the surface of the sea, we are welcomed into a peaceful oasis of quiet and stillness where the dining table takes center stage.

The quiet stillness takes us back to a time when Napoleon III encouraged growth and modernization in Normandy through infrastructure projects, including the construction of railways. This, together with Normandy's relative closeness to Paris and the attractions of Dieppe's and Le Havre's seaside resorts, brought an influx of new residents.

Among the new arrivals were many artists, attracted by the nature, the coast's light, and the beauty of the area. Painters like Turner, Courbet, Delacroix, Pissarro, and Renoir were fascinated by Normandy and its towns. For several decades, the Alabaster Coast, the Flower Coast, and the Mother-of-Pearl Coast, as well as Honfleur, Deauville, Trouville, Le Havre, and Mont-Saint-Michel, were their inspirations.

Perhaps the most important artistic development of the nineteenth century, Impressionism, was born in Normandy. The movement is named after Claude Monet's work *Impression, Sunrise*, painted in 1872 in his birthplace, Le Havre. One could say that Normandy and its coast were, throughout his life, his most important muse.

In the distance, less than thirty miles off the coast of Basse-Normandie, are the Chausey Islands, known as the French Channel Islands, and the better-known British Channel Islands. Both are part of the Duchy of Normandy. Known as The Bailiwick of Jersey and the Bailiwick of Guernsey, the Channel Islands remain independent; not part of the United Kingdom, or the EU, the islanders owe allegiance to the Duke of Normandy. So, notwithstanding the fact that she is a woman, they refer to Queen Elizabeth as "The Queen, our Duke" or, in French, "La Reine, Notre Duc."

As the candles are lit and the evening draws near, the fishing boats that dot the horizon remind us that Normandy does not end where the waves lap the rocks beneath us, but out there beyond the sea.

In this traditional table setting, the bread plate and the butter knife sit above the forks on the left side, while the water and wine glasses are placed at the top right of the dinner plate, above the knives.

The Kente cloth striped table cover provides a sophisticated backdrop for the table décor
and mirrors both the colors of the hand-painted flower dinnerware and the rural landscape.

Veal Escalopes
à la Normande

Serves 6

Ingredients

6 (5- to 6-ounce/141- to 170-g) veal cutlets
1 tablespoon sunflower oil
1 tablespoon Calvados
10 1/2 ounces (300 g) white mushrooms, cleaned
5 tablespoons (75 g) butter
1 2/3 cups (400 ml) heavy cream
2 tablespoons Dijon mustard
Salt and pepper
Cooked rice or potatoes and any green vegetable,
for serving

Preparation

Pound the veal cutlets to about a 1/4-inch
(6-mm) thickness.
In a large skillet, heat the sunflower oil over
medium heat and, when hot, brown the cutlets
on both sides, 2 to 3 minutes per side. You may
need to do this in batches.
When all of the cutlets are cooked, return
them to the pan and turn off the heat. Add
the Calvados. Set flame to the Calvados to
flambé and deglaze the pan. Keep the cutlets
in the cooking juices in the pan.
Peel the mushrooms and cut them in quarters.
In a medium skillet over medium heat, melt the
butter and fry the mushrooms. When most of the
juices have evaporated, add the cream, mustard,
and salt and pepper, stir thoroughly, and add to
the pan with the cutlets.
Turn the heat to low, cover the pan, and heat
the cutlets through for 2 to 3 minutes.
Arrange the veal on a serving platter topped
with the mushroom sauce.
Serve with rice or potatoes and any green vegetable.

168

Petit pois green peas, picked before full maturity, are a simple delicacy that bring
out the best in meat dishes. As they are smaller than normal green peas, and their
skins quite soft, they are also delicious when eaten raw or lightly cooked.

Fig Tart
Serves 6

Ingredients

1 sheet puff pastry, thawed
1/2 cup (120 g) black fig jam
1 1/2 pounds (750 g) ripe figs
1 cup (200 g) sugar
4 tablespoons (50 g) butter
1 cup (232 g) crème fraîche or vanilla ice cream,
for serving

Preparation

Preheat the oven to 325°F (160°C).
Line a 10-inch (25-cm) pie pan with parchment paper
and arrange the puff pastry dough to fit the pan. Pierce
the dough with a fork. Spread a thin layer of fig jam
over the dough.
Halve the figs lengthwise and arrange them very tightly
on the dough, skin side down. (You can peel the skin
off the figs if you prefer.) Sprinkle the sugar evenly on
top of the figs.
Cut very small cubes of butter and put one on top of
each fig. Bake the tart for 45 minutes to 1 hour, until
the juices have evaporated and the figs and dough are
browned. Remove from the oven. Slide off the parchment
paper. Serve hot with crème fraîche or vanilla ice cream.

A candlelit dinner on the edge of the sea is a magical experience; this is especially true when it takes place
in Normandy, a region that boasts more than three hundred miles of coastline. This geography has made
fishing a centuries-old tradition in Normandy, where generations have made their livings from the sea.

Sunflowers & Cactuses
Of Art & Food

Surrounding the exuberant décor of the dinner table, the combination of the geometries of modern art and the breathtaking blue of the southern Pacific Ocean that defines Chile's coastline, reveals the unexpected harmony of this interplay. Truly a feast for all the senses, the positioning and the décor used on the dining table unfold the broadest of horizons, where nature, human artifact, culinary presentation, and flavors all play a part.

Food is at the very center of life in France, as is art, which occupies a supreme place in the culture. These are two passions whose comingling has been the subject of much debate over the centuries—and one that knows no geographical bounds. In fact, food and art have carried on a global and, at times, unexpected and fanciful relationship.

Thousands of years ago, the Egyptians depicted crops, bread, fish, and other foodstuffs in hieroglyphics found on tablets and walls. In the 1500s, Giuseppe Arcimboldo painted whimsical, puzzle-like portraits in which facial features were composed of fruits, vegetables, and flowers. However, scholars have credited the Baroque master Caravaggio with a new artistic paradigm in which to view food. In his still life *Basket of Fruits* (1599), food evolves from object to subject. No longer merely form, it is now the protagonist of art.

On the other side of this debate, Chef François Pierre Sieur de La Varenne in his *Le Cuisinier François* (1651) equated the idea of French cooking with passion and its aspiration as a work of art. The cookbook was a bestseller of its day and reprinted across Europe thirty times in seventy-five years. In 1825, the noted French scholar and gourmand Brillat-Savarin extends its meaning and impact when he states: "Cooking is one of the oldest arts and one that has rendered us the most important service in civic life."

In 1913, Marcel Proust equated food with memory and used it to launch the narrative of *À la Recherche du Temps Perdu* (In Search of Lost Time), a seminal novel of the twentieth century. Twenty years later, Filippo Tommaso Marinetti published *The Futurist Cookbook*, where he depicted food preparation as part of a new worldview and entertaining as an avant-garde performance.

Since the 1960s and advent of pop art, both artists and chefs have continued to narrow the distance between our sensory realms. With countless perspectives, and an ever-evolving set of protagonists, it is no wonder that the French *art de la table* continues to fascinate minds and enrich our everyday lives.

Opposite "The pleasure of the table belongs to all ages, to all conditions, to all countries, and to all areas; it mingles with all other pleasures, and remains at last to console us for their departure."—Brillat-Savarin. *Following pages* Patterns and bold colors, both on the walls and on the table, create a visual balance that makes the space feel genuine and welcoming.

Opposite and Above The Ocean dinnerware is by Gien, the French faience manufacturer founded in 1821. This dinnerware extends our vision of the ocean outside the window by bringing to the table the wonders of the underwater world with a bold artistic statement. The marine theme of the embroidered linen placemats provides a continuation of the fresh color patterns that define both the china and the food presented.

Grilled Sole Fillets with Beurre Blanc

Serves 8

Ingredients

For the Fish
1 large (6 1/2 pound/3 kg) Pacific sole (or turbot)
without skin, cut into fillets
4 tablespoons (60 g) butter, sliced
Salt

For the Sauce
4 shallots, chopped
1 cup (250 ml) white wine, or Champagne
or Noilly-Prat vermouth
1 stick plus 6 tablespoons (200 g)
very cold butter, cubed

For Finishing
1 tablespoon olive oil
1 onion, sliced
2 large tomatoes, sliced
1 lemon, thinly sliced, for serving
Boiled potatoes and sautéed greens, broccoli,
or chicory, for serving

Preparation

Preheat the oven to 500°F (250°C).
Dry the fillets with paper towels. Grease an oven dish with
a little of the butter, then sprinkle on some salt. Place the
fish fillets on top. Dot the fillets with the remaining butter
and salt them.
Cook for about 15 minutes. Then, set the oven on broil
and brown the fish.

In a small pan, combine the shallots and the white wine.
Bring to a boil and reduce down to 1 tablespoon liquid.
Reduce the heat and incorporate the butter, one piece at a
time, while whisking constantly. The mixture will thicken.
Once all of the butter has been incorporated, pass the sauce
through a sieve over a bowl to remove shallots and serve
warm in a sauceboat with the fish fillets.

In a hot, nonstick pan with the olive oil, lightly sauté the
onion slices and tomatoes for 3 minutes, then arrange them
on your serving dish with the cooked fish fillets on top.
Arrange lemon slices around the perimeter of the dish.
Serve with boiled potatoes and sautéed greens, broccoli,
or chicory.

The simple and clean presentation of the fish fillets, which are surrounded by lemon slices
and laid on top of tomatoes and onions, is an unmistakable sign that summer has arrived.

In the Heart of Paris

An Evolving Passion

The French *art de la table* reached its most complex and elaborate pinnacle during the reigns of Louis XIV through Louis XVI. Today, although some long-held principles remain central to a successful repast, the possibilities for a successful staging are truly endless.

The ceremony known as the Royal Table, was an affirmation of the king's power and was held at 10 p.m. in the queen's or the king's antechamber. Nowadays, dinner is set at the time that is most suited to the lifestyle of the host or hostess and their guests. This is also true when deciding upon the location in which to dine.

Regardless of the occasion, it can be in a pantry, a sitting room, a library, a dining room, or outdoors, in a patio or garden, as all of these locations offer wonderful possibilities to capture one's imagination. At the table, the most impactful and central axiom to the mood created is the desired degree of contrast, or harmony, that one is striving for in the visual, the olfactory, and the spectrum of flavors chosen for the occasion.

Visual contrasts and surprises are central to entertaining— and rewarding for both the host and the guests. Whether choosing a wildly boisterous tablecloth and contrasting it with a solid-color napkin or vice versa, the rhythm and tonal quality of the tableware are elements of the silent musical score that underlies the gathering.

This search for the perfect aesthetic balance extends and guides the choice of dishes and glasses, whether modern or antique; today they can be mixed, if that is the host's preference.

The selection will have the best result when one has an eye for color and balance of the table décor and the food that will be served during the meal.

As far as the table décor, the only rule that has endured is that round tables are best suited to round table centerpieces and long tables are best enhanced when there is a longer table decoration with some symmetry applied.

Finally, and most important, the chosen elements that make up the menu are the final punctuation, the distillation of all that is the subject of the gathering. It is the language of the moment we will hold forever.

Among the many firsts that can be found in the annals of French culinary history is the Nicolas de Bonnefons book *The French Gardiner: Instructing How to Cultivate All Sorts of Fruit-Trees & Herbs for the Garden* (1651). This book, which he dedicated to women (*Dédié aux dames ménagères*), is the first treatise on household economy.

180

French cuisine is rooted in regional and foreign customs that date back over a thousand years. From the discovery of new crops and the adoption of precious foreign spices, from the migration of countless peoples and the return of its emissaries, it is a long, rich history that meanders through centuries of military conflicts and exploration. The impact of this history is everywhere in this home, which cultivates in equal measure French history and its culinary arts.

Opposite Gingham is woven so that the colored yarns go against the uncolored ones to create a lightweight texture that is also reversible. Dorothy in *The Wizard of Oz* immortalized it in its blue version in 1939. It was reimagined in 1965 by James Bond in *Thunderball*, when he wore a pink gingham shirt. This truly iconic five-hundred-year-old fabric is still a staple of summer picnics, of childhood memories, and of youth's power to enchant. Its impact is warm and immediate. *Above* Roasted baby potatoes are fun to eat and easy to cook. When combined with the côte de boeuf they add a touch of visual whimsy to this classic combination.

Côte de Boeuf

Serves 4

Ingredients

1 (2-pound/900 g) bone-in rib steak
Coarse sea salt

Preparation

Pat the beef with sea salt on both sides. Heat the broiler. Place the meat in an oven-safe pan. Place it in the oven about 3 inches (8-cm) below the broiler (leave the oven door open about 2 inches (5-cm). Cook for 8 to 12 minutes per side.

Béarnaise Sauce

Ingredients

2 sticks (250 g) butter
1 shallot, chopped
3/4 cup plus 1 1/2 tablespoons (200 ml) white wine vinegar
4 egg yolks
1 tablespoon chopped tarragon leaves
Salt and pepper

Preparation

Put the butter in a bain-marie or double boiler to clarify. Remove the impurities from the top, decant, and remove the whey from the bottom. Keep it warm.
In a small pan, combine the shallot and vinegar. Over medium heat, cook until the vinegar is reduced to about 1 tablespoon.
In a bowl over a bain-marie of simmering water set over medium heat, whisk the egg yolks with the shallot-vinegar reduction to obtain a sabayon or light custard.
Turn off the heat and slowly pour in the clarified butter while constantly whisking.
Add the chopped tarragon, season with salt and pepper, and serve.

184

A popular cut of beef in France, the côte de boeuf is a thick, bone-in rib steak.

Opposite and Above Dark blue is an unusual color for the theme of an entire dining table décor; however, surrounded by the warmth of the wood paneling the color brings a surprising tranquility to the space and delivers classic French elegance. In Bernardaud's subtle Eventail Bleu (Blue Fan) design, a trompe l'oeil effect is created by the use of a platinum-toned lace pattern set against the light and dark blue hues. The alternating Baccarat Harcourt Bleu and the Saint-Louis Tommy glasses create a wonderful geometry against the dark blue tablecloth.

Meringue Pavlova with Cream & Berries
Serves 8

Ingredients

4 egg whites, at room temperature
Pinch salt
1 cup plus 2 1/2 tablespoons (235 g) granulated sugar
2 cups (500 ml) whipping cream
2 tablespoons confectioners' sugar
1 cup (225 ml) mascarpone
Fresh strawberries and raspberries
Strawberry or raspberry sorbet (optional)

Preparation

Preheat the oven to 200°F (90°C). In a bowl with a hand-held beater or the bowl of a stand mixer with a whisk attachment, beat the egg whites until foamy.

Add a pinch of salt and continue to beat, adding 1 tablespoon of granulated sugar at a time and beating well after each addition, for about 15 minutes in total.

Once egg whites are whipped, place a sheet of parchment paper on a baking sheet.

Use a pastry tube fitted with a large plain tip to pipe the meringue into concentric circles on the parchment paper, starting at the center and continuing until you have used up the meringue.

Bake about 2 hours at 200°F (90°C), until the meringue is cream colored and firm.

Turn the oven off. Leave the meringue in the oven for several hours or overnight without opening the oven door. When ready to serve, carefully peel away the parchment paper. Whip the cream with the confectioners' sugar until firm. Fold in the mascarpone.

Put the meringue on a cake plate. Cover it by alternating and decorating with the whipped cream and red fruits and then add scoops of sorbet.

Note: You can also serve this dessert with a red fruit coulis.

New Zealand and Australia may never agree as to where the Pavlova was invented and by whom.
However, both agree it was named after the Russian ballerina Anna Pavlova, who toured
Australia and New Zealand in 1926.

On the Left Bank
Dancing Lilies & Dahlias

There is no doubt that the lively and timelessly elegant quarter that is the 7th arrondissement in Paris is the inspiration and the perfect setting for this refined table décor, conceived with minimal color and for maximum dramatic effect.

The juxtaposition of large geometric and freeform volumes that are placed on the table play a central role in the performance that will unfold, while the striking balance of darkness and light is the chosen rhythm on this night.

Further dramatic effect is achieved by the interplay of the glossy black surface with floral centerpieces that display extremely dark hues of crimson, purple, and black over the surface of the dark-brown-striped wood grain. Finally, the circular white background of the porcelain plates creates a virtual spotlight that puts center stage the brightly colored elements in the fresh langoustine salad.

The surface of the table is not just a space to be subdivided among a number of attendees; it is the field upon which we stage the performance, the play that will follow. Each element plays a role and must conform to its mission to create a balance that places functionality and form on the same plane as stylistic impact.

The shiny black placemats suggest to the guests that, although elegant, this is meant to be a casual affair. This statement is echoed with minimal cutlery laid directly on the glossy surface, to each side of the charger, or presentation, plates. The choice of this simple rectangular shape and the absence of color, even in the napkin, is deliberately chosen to highlight the dinner guests and the dishes presented.

The placemats are set in from the edge of the table and placed so as to create an appropriate distance between each guest. This regular rhythm allows for the geometric pattern of the contrasting plate to be the focus of attention, while the clear crystal glasses create a contemporary look of scattering arcs of white.

Set in one of Paris's most desirable, refined, and creative neighborhoods, the simple lines and the sharp contrasts are indeed the soloists in this dramatic performance. However, these ultimately relinquish the spotlight to the intricate dance of dark burgundy dahlias and black star calla lilies that erupt from the centerpiece of black vases.

Le Rouge et le Noir, Stendhal's iconic novel, with its plot that unveils passion and intrigue, and ultimately satire, could be the inspiration behind this setting.

192

Above The elegant and architectural lines evident in the Baccarat Harcourt design are unmistakable. The Harcourt was created in 1841 and is the oldest in the Baccarat line. Since the age of Napoleon III, this iconic glassware has been selected for use in the home of the president of the French republic, Palais de l'Élysée. *Opposite* The Ombrelle design of these bone-china porcelain plates by Compagnie Francaise de l'Orient et de la Chine is inspired by the ray arrangement of wires seen in traditional Japanese and Burmese umbrellas.

Sea Bass Ceviche

Serves 8

Ingredients

2 1/4 pounds (1 kg) fresh sea bass fillets
(or another white, nonfatty fish)
1 fresh green chili pepper
6 limes
1 tablespoon olive oil
Salt and pepper
1 red onion, sliced into thin strips
1 tablespoon chopped fresh cilantro/coriander leaves,
plus more whole leaves for garnish
1 head Bibb lettuce
2 medium sweet potatoes, boiled and sliced
2 ears corn, boiled, drained, and chopped
into 3 to 4 pieces each

Preparation

Cut the fish into 1- to 1 1/2-inch (2 1/2- to 4-cm) squares.
In a glass or metal bowl, rub the chili pepper on the inside,
to give the flavor. Slice the pepper into very thin pieces and
add to the bowl; it is very spicy.
Add the fish cubes and squeeze the limes over the fish.
The fish needs to be well covered. Add the olive oil, salt
and pepper, sliced onion, and the chopped cilantro.
Toss well.
Keep in the refrigerator for 20 minutes and serve on lettuce
leaves with the slices of boiled sweet potato and corn on the
cob. Garnish with cilantro leaves.

Opposite The brilliant natural hues of the lettuce, onions, and sweet potatoes are a wonderful complement to the dark and
high-contrast table décor. *Following pages* Silver was traditionally used as a material to reflect light at the dining table. Here
the Wedgwood Jasper Conran platinum espresso coffee service also adds a decidedly modern aesthetic to the table setting.

Chicken in Yellow Pepper Sauce

Serves 8

Ingredients

6 cups (1 1/2 l) chicken broth
2 whole chicken breasts, boneless and skinless
2 medium red onions, finely chopped
2 cloves garlic, minced
1/4 cup (60 ml) vegetable oil
1/2 cup (110 g) ají amarillo (yellow hot pepper) paste
1 teaspoon turmeric
1/2 teaspoon ground cumin
8 slices white bread, chopped,
or 15 water crackers, crumbled
1 cup (250 ml) milk
1 cup (250 ml) evaporated milk
1/2 cup (55 g) pecans or walnuts
1/2 cup (40 g) grated Parmesan cheese
Salt and pepper
Boiled potatoes, hard-boiled eggs, black olives,
and cooked white rice, for serving

Preparation

In a large saucepan, heat the chicken broth and, when hot, add the chicken breasts. Simmer gently, heat until cooked through, about 25 minutes.

When cooked, transfer the chicken to a plate and set aside the saucepan with the cooking liquid. Let the chicken cool, and then shred the meat and reserve.

In a pot, sauté the chopped onion and minced garlic in the oil until the onion is translucent. Add the ají amarillo, the turmeric, and the cumin. Let it simmer for about 2 more minutes.

In a blender combine the chopped bread, the milk, the evaporated milk, the nuts, and the Parmesan. Blend until smooth, adding some of the reserved stock to obtain a creamy consistency. Add this mixture to the pot with the onions and spices. Slowly mix in some additional broth, if necessary, to create a creamy consistency, and let cook for 5 minutes. Add the shredded chicken, stir gently, and heat until the chicken is just warmed through. Season with salt and pepper.

Transfer to a serving platter with the potatoes, hard-boiled eggs, and black olives. Serve white rice alongside.

The pairing of chicken and eggs is a surprisingly satisfying combination that is also a visual feast when accompanied with green salad.

Collecting Porcelain
Imperial White Gold

The French began arriving in Chile in the eighteenth century, setting themselves up as merchants, farmers, and shopkeepers. Today, Chileans who claim French ancestry make up the third-largest European community in the country, and include its former president Michelle Bachelet.

At this Santiago dinner table, the influence of the French aesthetic is unmistakable. The elegant vermeil and silver cutlery, the classical design of the crystal glassware, and the finest porcelain dinnerware are a visual cue to the hostess's aesthetic preferences, while the model of the schooner on the cabinet is a reminder of the maritime journey her ancestors undertook to reach these shores.

The unmistakable hallmarks of the French, English, and German porcelain laid out before us—featuring vitrified material and a white, fine-grained body—are very different from earthenware, whose surface would be porous, opaque, and coarser. The fabrication of porcelain started in China during the Tang Dynasty. However, it was not until the Yuan Dynasty, around the fourteenth century, that it evolved into the modern material with which we are familiar.

The word porcelain is derived from the Italian word *porcellana*, used to describe a cowrie shell that Marco Polo associated with the shiny pottery he found in China and brought back to Europe at the end of the thirteenth century. After its discovery, this fragile material became so highly prized that it even sparked a porcelain mania in 1603, when pieces sold at such high prices that porcelain was known as "white gold."

The first-ever European soft-paste porcelain was made in Florence in about 1575. However, it was not until 1707, at the Meissen factory in Saxony, that the secret to creating porcelain similar to that made in China was unlocked. Johann Friedrich Böttger is widely credited with this achievement, although some say it was his supervisor, the gifted mathematician Ehrenfried Walther von Tschirnhaus, who was instrumental in its discovery.

On this beautifully laid out dinner table, we see some of Meissen's fine workmanship in its most famous Onion Pattern design; two Aux Rois plates designed by Bernardaud, the renowned French porcelain master based in Limoges since 1863; and finally, a stunning example of the workmanship of Royal Crown Derby. The latter, originally established in 1750, is still creating fine bone-china tableware and giftware in its Osmaston Works factory in Derby, England.

In this city, not far from the shores of the great Pacific Ocean, the best of European ceramists play a leading role at this table as we celebrate our friends and this ancient craft, which was brought by an Italian across the world from China.

The pairing of the plates with the Carl Rotter blue crystal water glasses underscores the blue pattern in the chinaware. Meissen's Onion Pattern is the culmination of the search for a very special blue that would emphasize the white of the porcelain while still harmonizing with its tone.

Lamb Curry
Serves 6

Ingredients

1 cup (230 g) plain yogurt or cottage cheese
1 tablespoon grated fresh ginger
3 cloves garlic, crushed
1/4 teaspoon ground saffron
Salt
1/4 cup (60 ml) olive oil
3 onions, chopped
3 stalks celery, peeled and diced
1 green bell pepper, seeded and diced
1 teaspoon turmeric
2 tablespoons garam masala or yellow curry powder
2 teaspoons paprika
3 pounds (1 1/2 kg) lamb shoulder or leg,
trimmed and roughly chopped
1 cup (240 ml) coconut milk
Cooked basmati rice, mango chutney, chopped peanuts,
grated coconut, red chili paste, and sour cream with
fresh mint, for serving

Preparation

Place the yogurt in a bowl. Stir in the ginger, garlic, and saffron. Season with salt and set aside to rest for 3 hours.
Heat a Dutch oven over high heat with the olive oil.
Add the onions and cook, stirring frequently, until softened.
Add the celery and bell pepper and cook for 3 additional minutes. Add the turmeric, garam masala, and paprika and the lamb. Cook for 5 minutes.
Add the prepared yogurt mixture and the coconut milk and stir to combine.
Cover and simmer for 40 minutes over low heat, stirring occasionally.
Serve with rice and offer the other toppings on the side.

Preceding pages The pairing of Carrs's silver and gold Queen's cutlery with Bernardaud's Aux Rois plate is a perfect way to highlight the elegant design that was inspired by the grand French dining tradition. *Opposite* A selection of sweet, spicy, and savory sauces and steamed rice give this dish of curried lamb a welcome versatility. *Following pages* The fine Royal Crown Derby Midori Meadow plate displays a Japanese aesthetic that is well suited to the design pattern and subtle woven texture of the Jacquard Français tablecloth.

Above The fresh tones of the white wine and green crystal Baccarat glasses are echoed in the avocado salad, lifting the color palette substantially. *Opposite* China cabinets were first fashioned in the seventeenth century in England. They were designed to display expensive, imported fine china—highly prestigious objects to be showcased for all to see.

A Quiet Gathering

Joys of the Golden Room

Born of Italian curiosity, Dutch ingenuity, British ambition, and, ultimately, French love of freedom... New York City is a metropolis where everyone and everything is at home. Not so far above the city that never sleeps, yet a thousand light-years from the hustle and bustle of everyday life, we are transported into a golden oasis of quiet refinement. A timeless ritual is about to begin and a table is set.

The ormolu Empire candlesticks, the bow-backed chairs and inlaid table, the elegant dinnerware and silver cutlery— all are the distillation of centuries of technological evolution, and, by their careful selection, highlight how society prizes the tools chosen for such social interactions.

Indeed, over time the ritual of shared food saw us move from eating out of often beautiful and yet rough earthenware and glass vessels, to creating elaborate dinnerware pieces that are works of art, reflecting the highest craftsmanship as well as the imagination of generations of artisans and ceramists.

The fork and knife that we use today are relatively new, as we moved from purely utilitarian and rudimentary cutting tools to manufacturing glorious, jewel-like cutlery—the placement of which, no matter how simple the menu or numerous the components of the meal, conforms to both its chronological use and the side of the hand that will use the tool.

The fork was not widely adopted as a dining utensil in Europe until the eighteenth century.

Although the fork had been in existence since Ancient Greece, it was Catherine de' Medici, as queen of France, who made the fork a common sight at court in the sixteenth century. In the seventeenth century, a guest's individual knife was allowed at the table but its end had to be blunt and round. It is said that Cardinal Richelieu pushed for this innovation, not for fear of his life, but rather because he was annoyed by his guests picking their teeth with their knives.

Centuries later, and a continent away, we look upon the graceful inlaid marquetry table, the gold motif of the presentation charger, and the exquisitely painted Chinese phoenix design on the dinner plate and everything seems just as it should be. So, too, does the winged seraph smile as a gentle golden light advances the afternoon into evening.

By highlighting the striking candelabras the table setting is formal and yet contemporary,
and extends onto the dinner table the elegance and intimacy of this interior.

Opposite The classic ebony and silver salt and pepper mills recall a time when this precious wood was used to craft decorative objects as well as cabinets for the luxury trade. In Paris, the ebony cabinetmakers were known as *ébénistes*, the French term that is still used to describe the profession of cabinetmaker. *Above* The Mottahedeh Chelsea Bird porcelain plates are inspired by the designs of the workshop of James Giles and his birds of "distinctly disheveled appearance." The Pimpernel Old World Maps placemats are a perfect blend of masculinity and erudition. They complement the bronze and gilt Empire candlesticks and the striking porcelain tureen that replaces flowers on this elegant urban table.

Boeuf Stroganoff
Serves 6

Ingredients

1/4 cup (60 ml) vegetable oil
1 onion, finely chopped
2 cloves garlic, minced
1 tablespoon (14 g) butter
7 ounces (200 g) white mushrooms, quartered
14 ounces (400 g) beef tenderloin/fillet of beef,
cut into small cubes
1 teaspoon paprika
2 tablespoons cognac
2 tablespoons all-purpose/plain flour
2 cups (500 ml) beef broth
1 cup (250 ml) heavy cream
Salt and pepper
1/4 teaspoon grated nutmeg
Chopped parsley leaves, for garnish
Cooked pasta or white rice, for serving

Preparation

Heat half of the vegetable oil in a sauté pan. Add the onion and garlic and sauté until the onion is browned. In a separate sauté pan, melt the butter and add the mushrooms. Sauté, stirring occasionally, until the mushrooms are browned, for about 5 minutes.

In a large sauté pan heat the remaining 2 tablespoons of oil and brown the meat cubes in batches. Once all of the meat has been browned, add the sautéed onions and paprika. Turn off the heat, add the cognac, and flambé, swirling the pan until the flames subside. Turn the heat back on to medium, sprinkle in the flour, mix well, and add the beef broth, the sautéed mushrooms, and the cream. Season with salt and pepper and nutmeg. Stir and let cook for a few minutes for the flavors to come together.

Transfer the beef stroganoff to a serving platter, scatter with parsley leaves, and serve with pasta or white rice.

214

Boeuf Stroganoff is a Russian dish of sautéed pieces of beef that traces its origins to mid-nineteenth-century Russia. The preparation of the dish varies not only based on local adaptations, which involve the seasonings, but also in the manner in which the meat is cut: diced, cubed, or cut into strips.

Rue de Tournelles

An Intimate Yet Grand Affair

Everything that the eye can see in this richly decorated room on the Rue de Tournelles in Paris—from the candelabras on the table to the silk damask Récamier and the proportions of the doors—combines to create aesthetic harmony through complexity of form and materials. And, while the ornate ceiling of this *hôtel particulier* (private mansion) is a testament to the elegance of seventeenth-century life in the Marais, the large allegorical figure of Prudentia, or Wisdom, that dominates the space reveals the intellectual tone of this home.

This street of the Marais is named after the Hôtel de Tournelles, a collection of buildings that dated from the fourteenth century. Once home to the kings of France, the property included several buildings spread over some twenty acres as well as the Maison Royale des Tournelles that was the residence of the king. After the death of Henry II, his widow, Catherine de' Medici, sold the property and used the proceeds to finance the construction of the Tuileries Palace.

At the center of the room, the beautifully laid out oval dining table is an elegant and versatile option; it appears to occupy less space than a rectangle while allowing for more diners.

The shape is also well suited for a wide range of larger formal gatherings as it can be extended with an extra leaf.

One can easily imagine such long oval or rectangular tables in the mansions of the Rue de Tournelles, which were the residences of France's powerful elite such as Sully, Henri IV's great minister, and Marguerite Louise d'Orléans, wife of Cosimo III de' Medici, the Grand Duke of Tuscany.

Square rooms or salons of the Rue de Tournelles are better suited to square or round dining tables, which provide intimacy for a small number of guests, enabling them to carry on more casual conversations or delve into intellectual debates.

The salons of such renowned residents as Madame de Sévigné, Victor Hugo, and the poet Théophile Gautier would most assuredly have hosted such dinners. Gautier might have been speaking of this very room when he wrote: "Art is beauty, the perpetual invention of detail, the choice of words, the exquisite care of execution."

The rich blue of the sky that surrounds Prudentia seems to open a doorway into a peaceful and wiser world as she reminds the guests of the importance of historical perspective in handling life's difficulties, depicted here as a snake. The delicate floral pattern of the dinnerware is beautifully echoed in the antique silver cutlery handle design, while the delicate pale blue color of the plate creates a striking contrast with the tablecloth.

Terrine de Foie Gras Mi-Cuit

Serves 8

Ingredients

2 (1 pound/500 g) lobes raw foie gras
2 1/2 teaspoons fine sea salt
1/2 teaspoon sugar
1 1/4 teaspoons ground white pepper
3 tablespoons cognac
Brioche or sourdough toast, fig chutney, broth,
and Madeira gelatin cubes, for serving

Preparation

Soak the lobes in water for about 1 hour (the water should be body temperature).

Drain the lobes and lay them on a cutting board. Separate the lobes. Open the lobes with a small knife and remove as many veins as possible. Place the lobes in a dish.

In a small bowl, mix together the salt, sugar, and pepper. Season the lobes on both sides with this mixture. Sprinkle with cognac. Store, covered with plastic wrap (cling film), in the refrigerator for 12 hours.

Preheat the oven to 300°F (140°C). Compact the livers into a terrine mold. Place the mold in a pan and fill the outer pan with water coming halfway up the sides of the terrine. Bring the water to a simmer on the stovetop.

Cover the pan with aluminum foil and place the pan in the oven. When the liver has melted, about 15 minutes, remove it from the oven. Remove the terrine from the pan of water. Let it cool for at least 3 hours at room temperature. Gently stir the livers in the terrine. Allow the fat to rise to the top. Place the terrine, covered in plastic wrap, in the refrigerator for 24 hours (and consume it within the following 3 days).

To serve, remove the foie gras from the mold by dipping it in boiling water for 1 minute. Unmold the terrine onto a flat plate, then invert onto a serving dish so that the layer of fat is again on top. Refrigerate for 30 minutes. Slice the foie gras with a hot knife (dipped in boiling water before cutting each slice).

Serve with brioche or sourdough toast and fig chutney, broth, and Madeira gelatin cubes.

The best way to enjoy foie gras, which many consider a masterpiece of haute cuisine, is with a lightly toasted piece of bread with perhaps a few grains of fleur de sel de Guérande salt sprinkled on top. Although the French are the largest producers and consumers of foie gras today, it was the ancient Egyptians who were the first to relish this delicacy, procured from the ducks and geese of the Nile River. Over time they developed their own technique to fatten the geese, as evidenced in the necropolis of Saqqara, dating to around 2500 BC, where there is a painting that shows the force-feeding of geese.

The cohesive blue color story, from the dining table décor and antique tiles that line the walls, creates a soothing and yet exciting display. The gold highlights add a sense of opulent grandeur. Such large neoclassically designed jasperware vases, featuring delicate relief work, were first seen in the Wedgewood collection in the late 1700s. The choice of these subdued and yet impressive works of art deliberately leads the diner into observing every detail on the table, while also providing a delicate base for the bold blue wildflowers.

Veal Meatballs in Tomato Sauce
Serves 6

Ingredients

2 small red onions or 4 shallots, finely chopped
1 clove garlic, peeled and minced
3 tablespoons vegetable oil
2 pounds (900 g) ground veal
3 tablespoons breadcrumbs
1 cup (100 g) grated Parmesan
2 eggs, beaten
Leaves of 1 bunch flat leaf parsley, finely chopped
(about 1/2 cup)
Salt and pepper
1/4 cup (30 g) all-purpose/plain flour
3 tablespoons olive oil
3 cloves garlic, halved
1 16-ounce (500-g) can tomato purée or canned
peeled tomatoes and their juices, pureed, about
2 cups
Leaves of 1 small bunch fresh basil
1 teaspoon sugar (optional)
Fried polenta sticks, white rice, saffron risotto, pasta,
mashed potatoes, and sautéed spinach, for serving

Preparation

Cook the chopped onions and minced garlic in a skillet
with 2 tablespoons of vegetable oil until transparent but
not browned.

In a large bowl combine the veal, breadcrumbs, Parmesan,
eggs, cooked onions and garlic, chopped parsley, and salt
and pepper. Mix until well combined. Use your hands to
make small balls of about 1 1/4 inches (3 cm) in diameter
and place on a flat dish or board.

Dredge the meatballs in the flour and then, working in
batches, brown them in a skillet over medium heat in the
remaining 1 tablespoon oil, about 1 to 2 minutes on every
side. Set aside.

In a Dutch oven, heat the olive oil and add the halved
garlic, tomato purée, basil, and sugar, if using.

Simmer over low heat for 5 minutes, then add the browned
meatballs to the tomato sauce. Cover and simmer over
medium heat for 15 minutes.

Serve with fried polenta sticks, or white rice, saffron risotto,
pasta, mashed potatoes, and spinach.

*Note: These meatballs are equally delicious in a white wine sauce. Make
and brown the meatballs as in the recipe. In a Dutch oven, make a roux
by melting 2 tablespoons (30 g) butter and whisking in a scant 1/2 cup
(50 g) flour. Add 1/2 bottle white wine and 4 cups (1 l) veal or chicken
stock and simmer to thicken slightly, then add the browned meatballs along
with the finely grated zest and juice of 1 lemon. Cover and simmer the
meatballs in the sauce for 15 minutes.*

The origin of the meatball remains unknown, although the Persian kofta, a dish of ground lamb rolled into orange-sized balls and glazed
with egg yolk and saffron, appears in some of the earliest Arabic cookbooks. The dish likely arrived in Europe along ancient trade routes.

Le Marais

Where Time Is Stilled

Deep in the heart of Paris, there is a secret enchanted place where time has stopped. In the quiet corners of this magical domain, we are permitted to linger in our imagination within the walls of this mansion and extend our senses in the garden, enriched by the long Parisian spring.

These are riches we are given: the sound of the rustling leaves in the air or the animated laughter in the sitting room; the smell of the damp grass or the scent of cut roses in a silver vase; a ray of sunshine dancing on a carpet of daisies or gliding down along the silk curtains.

One can only pause this cascade of emotions long enough to realize that Paris lives in the private mansions of Le Marais. As Marcel Proust wrote: "Even though our lives wander, our memories remain in one place." These are the treasured gifts.

Home to the exquisite symmetry of Place des Vosges, Le Marais seems to hold within its streets and squares the whole trajectory of French history. The area, situated on the Rive Droite (Right Bank) of the Seine, spreads across parts of the 3rd and 4th arrondissements. Up until the thirteenth century, this swampy outlying area of Paris (its name means "the swamp") was a backwater. It became popular with the high aristocracy when Charles I of Anjou, the brother of King Louis IX of France, built his residence there.

After the French Revolution, the Place Royale was renamed Place des Vosges to commemorate the fact that the Department of the Vosges was the first to support a campaign of the Revolutionary army. Over time, the district fell into disrepair and was completely abandoned by the nobility—a reality underscored by the nearby construction of the Marché des Halles in 1890.

Today, Le Marais is once again an elegant and vibrant area of Paris, with mansions that house such jewels as the Musée National Picasso-Paris and Musée Carnavalet, as well as exquisite private dwellings.

This is a perfect backdrop for a dinner set in the most elegant tradition of the French *art de la table*. It is a timeless tableau that creates an inviting harmony of the finest linen textures, elegant silver dinnerware, and gilded crystal goblets.

The quiet composure of this simple setting for two, with its glasses
of red wine and oeuf au plat, speaks of intimacy and romance.

Turbot en Papillote
Serves 8

Ingredients

3/4 teaspoon (2 g) fleur de sel or other coarse salt
4 tablespoons (60 g) butter, cut into small cubes
1 whole turbot, gutted and scaled
Steamed potatoes and lime quarters, for serving

Preparation

Preheat the oven to 350˚F (180˚C).
Line a large baking pan with a very large sheet of aluminum foil (it will need to enclose the fish completely).
Place parchment paper on top of the aluminum foil.
Sprinkle about half of the salt and half of the butter cubes on the parchment.
Pat the fish dry with paper towels and place it in the baking pan.
Scatter the remaining salt and butter on top of the fish.
Place another piece of parchment paper on top of the fish.
Fold up the aluminum foil around the fish to enclose it completely in a packet.
Crimp the aluminum foil to seal.
Bake in the preheated oven until the fish is opaque, 20 minutes for a fish on the smaller end of the range and 30 minutes for a fish on the larger end.
Remove the fish from the oven and let it sit for 5 minutes.
Carefully remove the foil.
Skin the fish and fillet it. Arrange the fillets on a serving dish.
Serve with steamed potatoes and lime quarters.

Note: If you would like to make a sauce to accompany the fish, a mousseline sauce is a good choice. Make a Hollandaise and then fold in beaten egg whites to lighten. A sauce vierge is also an option: seed and chop fresh tomatoes and combine with chopped parsley, olive oil, and balsamic vinegar or lemon juice.

Opposite The magical mix of silver and gold of the candelabra, the vermeil tableware, and the ormolu centerpiece vases are beautifully complemented by green and white Haviland Bonneval dinner plates. *Above* Deciding whether to leave the skin on the fish or not is a question of personal preference, of the occasion, and of the type of fish one is serving. Salmon, branzino, sea bass, snapper, flounder, and mackerel are delicious with or without the skin. On this occasion, the skin has been removed to reveal the delicate color and pattern of the flesh.

A wonderful red wine aerates in a crystal decanter next to a silver water pitcher with a scrolled handle and a curved lip;
a bottle of crisp white wine cools in the ice bucket. This is the picture of quiet bliss found in an alfresco Paris supper.

Roses & Peonies
In the Garden of Delights

On this wonderful Chilean terrace that overlooks a resplendent garden, the summer sunshine brings to life the vibrant colors of the fragrant flower centerpieces. The luscious roses, carefully chosen for their particular shade of pink, complement the crimson glassware on one table and contrast with the vibrant green tablecloth on the other. All of the décor is very French.

In the 1500s, after the arrival of the Spanish in Viña del Mar (Vineyard of the Sea), the valley was divided into two large agricultural haciendas, but when the railroad connected nearby Valparaiso to Santiago, the small town prospered and soon became the place to be. Residents embraced a lifestyle that included elaborate social gatherings and elegant lunches and dinners.

Although European grapevines, Vitis vinifera, had arrived with the Spanish around 1555, the variety planted then was País. It was not until the nineteenth century that French immigrants and investors brought their knowledge, new techniques, and new varieties, such as Cabernet Sauvignon, Carmenère, Malbec, Merlot, and Sauvignon Blanc.

It seems that this remote coastal stretch of land beyond the Andes was destined to be the home to many of the French who immigrated here from 1840 to 1940. The vast majority came from southwestern France, especially from the Basque country, Gironde, and the regions situated between Duran, Gers, and Dordogne.

As the area's population grew in the nearby Casablanca Valley, the small vineyards multiplied and grew in prestige, thanks to a temperate Mediterranean climate and the favorable terrain provided by the coastal range of mountains that runs parallel to the Andes. Today it is best known for its Sauvignon Blanc, Chardonnay, and Pinot Noir.

For this gathering, dishes use a wide range of farm fresh produce and are chosen to enhance, not overshadow, the aromas and complexity of the Chilean wines. The meal ends with the best of the Taittinger offerings, the Comtes de Champagne Rosé. It is the perfect pairing with the raspberry and peach ice cream, and it is also a visual salute to the voluptuous pink peonies.

Roses in vivid shades of pink, fuchsia, and magenta are a joyful sight that echoes the mood of a summer day. Ice molds with flowers incorporated into them are used as bowls that keep the ice cream cool.

The Christofle Pompadour cutlery is the perfect complement to the classical lines of the Chelsea Bird plates
by Mottahedeh. The pale green Beauvillé tablecloth adds to the serenity of the setting. The pastel colors
of this multilayered dish make a beautiful presentation when it is cut into triangular wedges.

Vegetable & Ham Crêpe Cake
Serves 8

233

Ingredients

6 ears corn, shucked
4 large tomatoes
1 pound (500 grams) thinly sliced baked ham
1 pound (500 g) runner beans
Salt and pepper
8 to 10 savory crêpes
2 cups (460 g) mayonnaise
1 cucumber, shaved with a vegetable peeler,
or 1 ripe avocado, peeled, pitted, and sliced

Preparation

Fill a large pot with water, bring to a boil, and cook the corn for 4 minutes. Drain and set aside to cool. When the corn is cool enough to handle, run a sharp knife shallowly down the side of one cob, then repeat so that you remove the kernels and halve them at the same time. Repeat with remaining corn.
Peel and seed the tomatoes. Cut the tomatoes into small cubes and drain. Cut the ham into dice.
Cut the runner beans into thin strips. Bring a pot of salted water to a boil, boil the beans for 5 minutes, then drain and allow to cool.
Season the corn, tomatoes, ham, and runner beans with salt and pepper but keep separate.
Place one crêpe on a large cake plate. Spread some mayonnaise on the crêpe, then add a half of the ham. Cover with another crêpe. Spread more mayonnaise on top and then add half of the beans. Cover with another crêpe, spread some mayonnaise on it, and add half the corn. Cover with another crêpe spread with mayonnaise, and top with half of the tomatoes. Repeat this process in the same order and then coat the top and sides of the stack with the remaining mayonnaise, spreading it thinly with an offset spatula. Keep refrigerated and serve cold. Garnish with the cucumber or avocado.

Above Savory layered crêpe cakes, served cold, are perfect for hot summer days. *Following pages* The visual impact of the olive-colored tablecloth is both tamed and highlighted by the Mottahedeh Vista Alegre Magnolia & Birds dinnerware, a fine example of Portuguese porcelain produced by this famed company, which traces its history back to 1824.

Roasted Pork Ribs
Serves 8

Ingredients

2 tablespoons vegetable oil
1 tablespoon white wine vinegar
2 tablespoons red-hot chili sauce
4 cloves garlic, crushed
2 teaspoons dried oregano, ground
Salt and pepper
2 racks pork ribs
1 cup (250 ml) white wine or water

Preparation

In a small bowl, mix 1 tablespoon of the oil with the vinegar, chili sauce, garlic, oregano, and salt and pepper. Use your hands to rub this mixture evenly over the pork ribs.
Preheat the oven to 400°F (200°C).
Place the ribs and the remaining mixture into a large, shallow roasting pan.
Cover with foil and bake for 35 minutes. Remove the foil from the tray and bake the ribs for another 45 minutes, turning them a couple of times, until the sauce has caramelized.
Add the white wine and use a wooden spoon to stir in the caramelized bits in the pan. This will make the sauce.
Roast for another 5 minutes. Transfer the ribs to a carving board and the sauce to a bowl.

Bean Purée
Serves 8

Ingredients

1 onion, finely chopped
2 tablespoons olive oil
2 15- or 16-ounce (500-g) cans cannellini or other white beans, rinsed and drained, or 3 cups (1 kg) shelled fresh white beans
Salt
2 tablespoons butter

Preparation

Sauté the onion in a large saucepan with the oil until translucent. Add the beans and sauté for 5 minutes.
Then add boiling water to cover the beans by 2 inches (5 cm). Boil for 20 minutes, stirring often.
Add salt and let the beans cook for another 10 minutes.
When the beans are soft and very little liquid remains, purée them with an immersion/stick blender. Add the butter and mix well.

Pebre Sauce
Makes 3 cups

Ingredients

1 cup (25 g) chopped flat-leaf parsley leaves
1 cup (25 g) chopped cilantro/coriander leaves
1 cup (100 g) chopped scallions/spring onions
1 cup (200 g) diced fresh tomatoes
2 tablespoons red wine vinegar
1 tablespoon ají verde (green hot pepper) paste
(or 1/2 cup chopped mild chilies)
1/4 cup (60 ml) vegetable oil

Preparation

Mix all ingredients in a bowl and serve with pork and bean purée.

Chilean pebre sauce is a variation of fresh salsa, with a flavor that provides the perfect contrast with grilled meats or fish. The heat in the condiment comes from Chilean ají verde.

238

Above The pinks of the floral centerpieces and glass tumblers are intended to bring out the many tones of green and enliven the table setting and dining terrace. *Opposite* Serving ice cream in an ice bowl helps keep it cool on a summer day.

The Dream of Zapallar
Ovalle & Brillat-Savarin

240

Zapallar is a picturesque coastal town in Chile. One highlight is a small rock cove sheltering a beach, where the prevailing sounds are those of nature and the sea.

Flanked by the ocean and the hills of the Chilean Coastal Range that runs from north to south along the Pacific, Zapallar has been described as the prettiest beach town in Chile.

Founded in the late 1800s by Olegario Ovalle, a wealthy landowner with a vast swath of land in the area, the seaside resort town is the result of Ovalle's 1892 gift of parcels of land to his friends. The condition: they had to build houses "in good taste." And so they did...

Many of his friends had traveled extensively in Europe, so the houses they built reflected that aesthetic influence. Ovalle himself brought back from his European travels both materials and skilled laborers to build his home.

Whether it be the mild climate, the vegetation, or the decidedly European flair of the beautiful homes, one is reminded of France, where many Chileans trace their ancestry.

The French gastronome Jean Anthelme Brillat-Savarin shared Ovalle's interest in the notion that "taste" in food, music, literature, and art was something objective that educated people could share and agree on. Indeed, this shared idea of "taste" connected the new international leadership, which transcended birth and geography.

Published in Paris in 1825, after Brillat-Savarin spent thirty years refining his thinking, the book *Physiologie du Goût* (The Physiology of Taste) argues his case for the importance of "taste" through witty anecdotes and reflections on everything gastronomical. He succinctly put it in the now famous dictum: "Tell me what you eat, and I will tell you what you are."

In the era that followed bicontinental political revolutions, unprecedented social upheaval, and the establishment of the bourgeoisie, Olegario Ovalle and Brillat-Savarin both understood the changes afoot.

They knew that a shared code and a common language called "taste"—and not birth—would unite and define the emerging social class.

Jean Anthelme Brillat-Savarin posited that culinary excellence was based not on transitory fashion but on the intrinsic quality of the ingredients and the care with which they were prepared.

243

Chilean Carbonada Meat & Vegetable Stew

Serves 6

Ingredients

2 1/4 pounds (1 kg) rump roast
3 medium or 2 large carrots
4 large potatoes, peeled
9 ounces (250 g) string beans
1/4 cup (60 ml) vegetable oil
2 medium onions, chopped
3 cloves garlic, chopped
Salt and pepper
1/2 teaspoon ground cumin
1/2 teaspoon ground coriander
1/2 teaspoon paprika
1/2 teaspoon dried oregano
2 cups (400 g) 1/4-inch diced butternut squash
or pumpkin
1 cup peas
Kernels from 2 ears corn
Minced cilantro/coriander and parsley
1 jalapeño or other chili pepper, thinly sliced (optional)

Preparation

Cut the meat cut into 1/4-inch cubes. Dice the carrots and potatoes into 1/4-inch cubes. Chop the string beans into 1/4-inch lengths.

Heat the oil in a Dutch oven and brown the meat for 3 minutes.

Add the onions and garlic and cook, stirring frequently. When the onions are transparent season with salt, pepper, cumin, ground coriander, paprika, and oregano.

Add the carrots and cook, stirring frequently, until they begin to color.

Add the potatoes and the squash.

Add boiling water to cover by several inches and simmer briskly over medium heat for 10 minutes.

Add the string beans, the peas, and the corn and cook until potatoes are soft enough to be pierced easily with a fork, about 5 additional minutes.

Top with cilantro, parsley, and chili pepper.

244

Preceding pages The graphic elements in the Kings design cutlery include a honeysuckle and a shell. These create an elegant statement and extend the richness of Spode's Shima dinnerware. *Opposite* The Chilean version of the traditional beef stew gets its flavor and texture from a variety of vegetables, including corn, potatoes, pumpkin, and carrots.

246

Choosing a palette dominated by mulberry, plum, and eggplant tones allows the dinnerware
to take center stage. The artistic skill and the imagination evident in the Gri-Gri dinner
service by Gien is inspired by the work of artist Valérie Dawlat-Dumoulin.

Chicken Breast with Tomatoes & Olives
Serves 6

Ingredients

1 clove garlic, pressed
Finely grated zest and juice of 2 lemons
1 tablespoon finely chopped flat-leaf parsley
Salt and pepper
3 tablespoons olive oil
2 whole chicken breasts, skin-on, bone-in
20 cherry tomatoes
20 green olives, pitted
3 shallots or 2 red onions, peeled and sliced
Olive or mushroom risotto, cooked white rice,
vegetables, or potatoes, for serving

Preparation

Preheat the oven to 350°F (180°C).
In a large bowl, mix the garlic, lemon zest, lemon juice,
parsley, salt, pepper, and olive oil.
Add the chicken breasts and rub with the seasoning mixture.
Then arrange the breasts in a roasting pan. Add the cherry
tomatoes, olives, and shallots around the chicken breasts.
Place in the oven. After 15 minutes check for moisture in the
bottom of the pan. If it is dry, add 1/2 cup (120 ml) of water.
Cook in the oven for 25 to 30 minutes. Once cooked, slice
the chicken breasts with a carving knife. Arrange on a serving
dish with the tomatoes, olives, and onions around.
To make a sauce: Add a cup of water to the roasting pan and
scrape the bottom to remove and dilute the caramelized bits
stuck on the pan. Warm the pan juices over medium heat,
then drizzle on the chicken breasts.
Serve with risotto, rice, vegetables, or potatoes.

248

Opposite The plum-colored Jacquard Français tablecloth is the canvas on which a tall centerpiece of plums, cherries, and artichokes
celebrates the seasonal bounty of nature. *Following pages* The refined taste of the classically French décor of the room, with its
golden tones, is extended onto the dining table with the ochre Jacquard Français tablecloth. The silver and turned-wood
candlesticks and Bernardaud's Prince Bleu Limoges china provide additional elements that add color and form.

Above The Savarin ring mold was first used in the nineteenth century to make the Julien brothers' gâteau Savarin. The Parisian pastry chefs named the cake after Brillat-Savarin, who gave them the recipe for the rum syrup used in the cake. Today the mold is used for sweet and savory dishes.

Salmon Ring Cake with Mustard Sauce

Serves 8

Ingredients

Butter for greasing the mold
4 tablespoons all-purpose (plain) flour,
plus more for the mold
2 pounds (900 g) fresh salmon fillets, skin-on
4 eggs
1 teaspoon baking powder
2 cups (500 ml) milk
1 cup (250 ml) heavy cream
1/2 cup (100 ml) vegetable oil
7 ounces (200g) Gruyère cheese, grated
1/2 bunch of fresh dill or 2 teaspoons dry dill weed
Salt and pepper
French fries or salad, for serving

Preparation

Preheat the oven to 400°F (200°C). Butter and flour
a 9-inch/23-cm cake or silicone mold.
Poach the salmon for 3 minutes in fish court bouillon,
or steam it. When cool enough to handle, crumble
the fish into small bits with your hands, removing
and discarding the skin and bones.
In a large bowl, whisk the eggs, then add the 4 tablespoons flour and the baking powder. Stir in the milk,
the cream, and the oil, and mix well. Add the grated
cheese, salmon, and dill, and season with salt and pepper.
Pour the salmon mixture into the prepared mold.
Bake for 40 minutes, or until a thin knife inserted
into the center comes out clean.
Remove from the mold when still hot and serve
with mustard or caper sauce.
To make the sauce: Mix heavy cream with Dijon
or English mustard to your taste.
Alternatively, you can mix the cream with capers,
and salt and pepper, and heat.
Pour over the salmon ring or serve alongside in a sauceboat.
Serve with French fries or a salad.

We may never discover if this is the same recipe for Salmon à la Brillat-Savarin that was served on February 22, 1913,
in the dining salon of the SS Victoria Luise as it sailed the Pacific. However, we do know that at 8:45 p.m. that same
day the passengers enjoyed a talk by Professor Monsen on the topic of the Panama Canal. So, as we savor this
delicate dish we can certainly close our eyes and imagine ourselves on that steamship voyage of long ago!

Acknowledgments

The inspiration for this book is the wonderful and ever-changing cast that comes together for family dinners that go past midnight; the friends who gather for supper during languid summer evenings, and the protagonists who enliven and lead the charge in boisterous lunches that reach into the afternoon; time capsules where conversations flow and the aroma of each course opens a new chapter of the meal. Without these leading actors playing their part in these staged encounters, this book would not have been possible.

The great hosts and hostesses of the past, whose craft still informs the vocabulary of the art of entertaining, are well and truly an encyclopedia of manner and style; their names may be forgotten to most but their role in molding this book is indisputable.

The great designers, innovators, and craftsmen whose work in glass, crystal, silver, and china grace these pages are the maestros. Their work is both the melody and the art in every table setting. Whether modern or traditional, elegant or casual, day or evening, large gathering or romantic supper, in elegant dining rooms or under an apple tree, theirs is the greatest of gifts: beauty in the service of life's most intimate gestures.

The masters of etiquette, who for centuries have endeavored to distill the utmost serenity and elegance in all manner of gatherings, are present in all that is portrayed in this book. That is the great gift that Mark Roskams contributes. Through his beautiful and revealing photography, he reads and conveys the subtlest of these clues in each fold of table linen; in each sumptuous glimmer of light reflected in a crystal glass. His interiors are stunning and his elegant photography is the very heart of this project.

No location was better than another—as each revealed an intimate setting, a wonderful garden, or a gracious home that allowed us to explore the possibilities that each gathering and each occasion offered.

Among the generous friends who opened their homes are Maki Miro Quesada and Monica Vidal in East Hampton; Laurence Coste in London; architect Frank de Biasi, Lavinia Branca, Cecilia Cuissart de Grelle, Sterling Hamill, Alexandra Kauka, Bonnie Pope, and Susana de la Puente in New York; Gerard Baignères, Yolaine Baignères, and Catherine Bernardin in Normandy; Ruben Alterio, Judith Aubry, Edouard Carmignac, and Il Marchese Federico Spinola in Paris; Sir Benjamin Slade, 7th Baronet, in Somerset; Monica Noel and Martine Schaeffer in Southampton; Alejandra Bunster, Carolina Garib, Patricia Ready, Josefina Sutil, and Edgardo Von Schroeders in Zapallar; and, of course, at the Château de la Marquetterie, our deep thanks go to Clovis Taittinger.

A very special thank you is owed to Emmanuel Bonneau, Belinda Briones, Claudio Chamorro, Patricia Diaz, Isabel Fuentes, Anita Garling, Enrique Lazcano, Rosa Montalvan, Etienne Roblot, Rolando San Martin, Luis San Jorge, and Alicia Soto, for their invaluable help, and also to the staff of Château de la Marquetterie, whose attention to detail is unparalleled.

We would also like to acknowledge the invaluable role of our project director Cristina Rizzo and Rizzoli editor Daniel Melamud: their keen eye and sensitive guidance made it all possible.

And finally, but foremost, to Michel Taittinger, for his unwavering support of this project.

254

The portrait of Jacques Cazotte hangs in the dining room
of Château de la Marqueterie, his former home.

First published in the United States of America in 2020 by
Rizzoli International Publications, Inc.
300 Park Avenue South
New York, NY 10010
www.rizzoliusa.com

Copyright © 2020 Claudia Taittinger
Text by Lavinia Branca Snyder
Photography by Mark Roskams
Art direction by Cristina Rizzo

Publisher: Charles Miers
Editor: Daniel Melamud
Design: Geoffrey Dunne
Copyeditor: Tricia Levi
Proofreader: Natalie Danford
Production Manager: Alyn Evans

Printed in China

2020 2021 2022 2023 / 10 9 8 7 6 5 4 3 2 1

ISBN: 9-780-8478-6224-5
Library of Congress Control Number: 2020935301

Visit us online:
Facebook.com/RizzoliNewYork
Twitter: @Rizzoli_Books
Instagram.com/RizzoliBooks
Pinterest.com/RizzoliBooks
Youtube.com/user/RizzoliNY
Issuu.com/Rizzoli